101 WAYS
TO TELL THE WORLD
TO KISS YOUR ASS

DAVID H. SCOTT

Take what works!
leave the rest!
David H. Scott

CONTENTS

———————

DEDICATION

I want to dedicate this book to my four children.

Cameron, Angie, Chrissi and Lavonne.

What great kids they have been and have turned out to be.

If only I could go back and do it all over again,
I missed so much of their lives growing up
and as young adults.
I love each and every one of you
more than words or deeds could ever let you know.

. . .

CHAPTER 1

1. Nothing lasts forever.

CHAPTER 2: PERSONAL

2. Make a Life's Plan, Just Like a Business Plan.

3. Know where you have been, where you are and where you are going.

4. Get in control of your life.

5. Suspect anything and everything.

6. Make up your own mind on everything.

7. Watching TV is a waste of time.

8. Reading the newspapers is a waste of time.

9. Do not do anything you do not want to.

10. Do not let people take an advantage of you.

11. Look out, if you just said "Yes."

12. Learn to say "NO."

13. Do what you want.

14. Go where you want.

15. Have several hobbies.

16. Look for ways to help others.

17. Above all else, be yourself.

18. If you need advice; seek it and then advise yourself.

19. Learn to entertain yourself.

20. No one is going to take care of you when the time comes but you.

21. Be prepared for anything.

22. Prepare for the future.

23. Listen to your soul and your spirit.

24. Get spiritual.

25. Have a sense of humor.

26. You don't usually change who you are because you want to. You change who you are because you have to.

27. Happiness is somewhere between too much and not enough.

28. When the time comes, there is no getting a 2nd chance.

29. When is enough, enough?

30. You know right from wrong.

CHAPTER 3: HEALTH

31.   Get healthy.

32.   Eat right.

33.   Do not smoke.

34.   Do not drink alcohol.

35.   Do not chew.

36.   Go for a walk daily.

37.   Exercise daily.

38.   Take some time for yourself.

39.   Treat your mind and your body if it were
        the only one you will ever have. It is!

CHAPTER 4: WORK

40. Pick a career early on in life that hopefully is the right one.

41. Start a small business.

42. Always show up to work early. Be the last one to leave.

43. Working is the key to making you "Free"…
    Plan-Plan-Plan.

CHAPTER 5:
FAMILY & RELATIONSHIPS

44. Think very hard before becoming a wife/husband
     or a mother/father.

45. Respect each other.

46. Have a deep expression of appreciation.

47. The success of the "Life's Plan" as well as the "Marriage
     and Relationship" is attributable to both parties.

48. There should be a spiritual connection.

49. Both agree the relationship takes constant work
     and attention.

50. Be who you are.

51. Enjoy being with yourself.

52. Are we having fun yet?

53. Loving each other is not going to be enough.

54. Having children is a huge responsibility.

55. Chances are whatever it is you think right now
     is a big deal, in a short period of time it won't make
     any difference.

56. You must have a healthy communication.

57. Both of you must have the same vision of success and agree on what the definition of "Free" is.

58. You both need a positive outlook on life.

59. You must trust each other.

60. Find simple.

61. You certainly don't need to spend all your time together.

CHAPTER 5: PLAY

62. Find what makes you want to do it again, then keep doing it.

63. Go walking.

64. Go hiking.

65. Go camping.

66. Play as hard or harder than you work.

67. Go kayaking, canoeing paddle boarding, bike riding.

68. Learn to paint.

69. Learn to play a musical instrument.

CHAPTER 6: FINANCIAL

70. If you don't owe any money, you are "Free."

71. Save 20% of every gross dollar you make.

72. Get your finances organized.

73. Demand your money's worth on everything.

74. Do not bank with a bank.

75. If you have too...file bankruptcy.

76. Use credit cards only for emergencies, car rental and pay them off monthly.

77. If you buy a home, only get a 15-year mortgage.

78. No car payments.

79. Never lease a car.

80. No RV payments, no boat payments, no furniture payments.

81. Get your fico score up to 750 plus and keep it there.

82. Do not live on credit.

83. Pay cash for everything.

84. Ride the bus.

85. Walk whenever you can.

86. Quit going out and eating. It is a huge waste of money.

87. Quit buying those expensive coffees.

88. Buy used if it works, fits or looks good.

89. Try to spend a year and not buy anything new.

90. Start an LLC or two to lessen your tax burden.

91. Start a second small business.

92. Do not be ignorant of the tax codes.

93. Do not pay for a service if you can do it for yourself.

94. Give yourself a raise by cutting out all the money you waste…and at the same time ask your boss for a raise.

95. Shop for your insurances and understand what you are committing to.

96. Renting sometimes can make more financial sense than buying.

97. Get efficient.

98. If you haven't touched it in a year, you never will…sell it, give it away or throw it away.

99. Think about the decision to spend an unusual amount of money before you do for 24 hours.

100. Remember this every day; someone out there is trying to take every dime you have.

101. Happiness and being "Free" are a state of mind!

INTRODUCTION

The idea of this book started in 2008. I was living up on 157 acres on East Lake, in Newberry Crater National Monument on some private property South of Bend, Oregon. My two brothers Jeff, Steve and I have a small percentage of ownership each in this property.

I spent 2 ½ years living in the cabin and a tipi on the property thru two winters. I would go to town approximately every three weeks. I loved to snowshoe out and back or take a snowmobile the 14-mile round trip to the locked gate. There was 10 feet of snow the 1st year and 8 ft of snow the 2nd year.

What struck me daily was how "Free" I felt. One could hear the silence. You could hear the birds singing for a mile. Not once did I get bored. There was no TV, by choice. In fact, to this day I don't watch TV at all. I contribute my "good health" to not watching TV and giving me the time to do the tremendous variety of things I do daily.

One of the great benefits of finally getting sober at the age of 50 in 1997 was the "Happy, Joyous and Free" life I have been gifted. It still took me six months to quit drinking after my 9th DUI. I am not proud of any one of the DUI's, but they happened. I am proud of the fact I finally got it.

I was getting a chance to experience these feelings for the 1st time in my life   Happy I could relate to. I don't think I am or ever have been a very "Happy" person. However, "joyous" was also something that I could relate to. There were many days up at the lake during this time I would get tears in my eyes from the over whelming experience I was "enjoying" of being in such a beautiful environment on a continual basis.

"Free" was an entirely different emotion, an experience I struggled with. Was I really "Free"? "Free" from what?

Webster's definition of "Free" is:

> 1. adj. not subject to external constraints or domination. Not captive, at liberty, able to move, loose, not having to be paid for, clear of a specified condition, not busy, without prior engagements, not reserved or occupied, not being used, unhampered, able to act and choose for oneself, spontaneous, voluntary. There are others, but you get the idea.

What an accomplishment I thought it would be to be really figure out how to be "Free." Free from debt. Free from the aspect of "work." Work when you want to, do what you want to do, not because you must. Have just enough money to do what one really wants. Live simply for the moment but have a plan that extends out for the future. Have someone in your life to do the things you truly want and them also want to do the same things. Be healthy. Go where you want to. Do what you want to do. In other words, get to experience life to the fullest.

Isn't that what each one of us truly wants? It is a fact. Few get to experience anything remotely close to living a fulfilled life or getting to be "Free" and truly being happy.

A lot of people wait until they retire thinking they will be "Free." A lot ride the work horse right to the mortuary or the fire. A lot of these retirements don't go to well. That is because they have no experiences or anything they can relate to that allows them to be "Free."

I started to realize that for my sobriety and my life to have any meaningful substance to it, I had to live on a daily basis. Not get too strung out in the future on the "what ifs" and for sure to not dwell on the past. I knew I needed to make sure I didn't spend too much time thinking on all the mistakes and bad decisions I had made. If only "I would have done it this way" of thinking. My God, why did I do that, that way? Boy, was that a life changing bad decision! Not the kind of thinking that is conducive to being emotionally or physically healthy. This sort of thinking also makes for tough sleeping at night. It certainly doesn't allow one to have any experiences or feelings of being "Free."

I was not a good husband or father. It has haunted me for years and does to this day. The longer I am sober, the freer I feel and the better my life gets. But in those two areas of my life I am beginning to realize just how extremely deficient I was on how to be a good husband and father.

Where did that come from? I don't have any idea.

But as I pondered the "Free" aspect of my life, I got to thinking up on Paulina Peak that 1st winter wouldn't it be fun? Wouldn't it be the greatest accomplishment in life to be able to get into a position:

"To Tell the World to Kiss Your Ass" and just be "Free."

Since then I have been on a quest to come up with my own definition of "Free", hence the book:

101 Ways to Tell the World to Kiss Your Ass.

I am 72 years old. Just another normal guy getting older every day by myself in life. I just read this morning that some of us are now being called "orphaned seniors." I can assure you, being alone was not my number one choice at this stage in the journey. But as my wife Debbie says (I can't stand to call her my Ex wife) as well as Jim Finch used to say and as my good buddy Ernie Feavel says, "It is what it is."

But there is one thing I am not sitting around waiting to do. That is dying.

Do I have anything to contribute? One would think so living 72 years as someone who has consistently lived life to the fullest. You would think there is some "experiences" I can share that are worthwhile. Share some of this thinking that would greatly benefit someone who is much younger. Somebody ought to find something out of "101 Ways" at any age that would greatly benefit their lives.

I am not an old 72 years old by any means. Most days I feel a good sound 45 or 50-years-old.

I completed in 2016 a 3000-mile kayak trip down the Yellowstone River, starting at Gardiner, MT to the Missouri River at Williston, ND and then down the Missouri to St. Louis, MO, and then down the Mississippi to Baton Rouge, LA. I started this trip on April 11, 2016 just below Gardiner, MT and made it 2,200 miles to Herman, MO, where I caught a virus and had to halt the trip on June 18. I resumed the trip on Oct 14, 2016 and completed the trip to Baton Rouge on November 17, 2016.

I just finished 1600 miles on the from Whitehorse, Yukon to the Native Village of Grayling, Alaska, short 250 plus miles of my goal Emmonak about 16 miles off the Bering Sea. My thumbs and thumb joints gave out on me. The pain was too much, I wasn't having any fun.

I certainly don't plan on stopping my long-distance kayak trips.

Mid May in 2019 I plan on going to Mongolia, kayak the shore line of Lake Khovsgol. Then paddle down the Eg

River to the Selenga River into Lake Baikal in Siberia 600 plus miles. Then paddle the1,200 miles of shoreline of Lake Baikal a total distance of 2,000 plus or minus miles. Lake Baikal is the largest volume fresh water lake in the world.

Then I have my sights on the MacKenzie River in the NW Territories and the Inland Passage from Bellingham, Washington to Skagway, Alaska. Does this sound like a 72-year-old guy sitting around waiting to die? No way.

So, listen up.

These kayak trips are a great way to experience the "Free" thing. To be sure, there were plenty of opportunities to "bend over" and give the world the "O Brown Eye" on any one of the trips I have taken. What a joy to do so.

The question must be asked? Do I have anything significant to contribute in the way of experiences that could benefit someone else, younger or older that still is struggling with life? I think so.

I have had a very full life up until now.

Numerous businesses, some successful but none ever lasted long.

Way too many jobs.

Several bankruptcies both personal and business.

Moved continually.

A drinker until 50.

9 DUIs.

A smoker until 51.

Didn't have a clue what "healthy" meant until 53.

A form of Prostate Cancer that they tell me won't kill me, I don't even think about it.

A great Entrepinuer but a lousy business man.

A terrible husband both times.

Not a good father. In fact, a majority of the time an "absentee father."

Spent 26 months in Vietnam, 19th, 20th and 21st birthdays.

Experienced combat with the 101st Airborne.

Learned invaluable life's experiences from Lt. General Rosson as his driver and personal aide.

Finally diagnosed with 100% Service Related PTSD, "Permanent and Decisive."

Very few friends over the years.

Ah... but let's not let most of the above be all doom and gloom. Fact of the matter is I have learned to benefit from all of that "adversity" and perception of doom and gloom. I lead a pretty envious life most of the time.

I don't know about you if you are lucky enough to be a healthy 72, but all but a couple of the few friends I did have are dead. A couple of them drank themselves to death. A few passed because of cancer. I learned after Vietnam to not get to "attached" to anything or anybody because the relationships just didn't seem to last very long.

The title: ***101 Ways to Tell the World to Kiss Your Ass*** was meant to be catchy. It could indicate a sense of humor in the contents. That construed would be completely the opposite of my intentions. The core theme of this book is very serious. This day and age with all the challenges going on in the world, the huge amount of stress of day to day living, raising a family, working a job, the struggle to just survive, you, me and anyone of us can use all the "experience, wisdom, been there...done that we can get."

I can tell you this. If I would have just had an inkling of what I posses now in wisdom, experience from the successes and failures, I would have had the opportunity to be "Free" a long time ago.

There are three 3 things that I believe are absolute to getting "Free" sooner than later. Do I wish somebody would have

sat me down when I got out of Vietnam and drilled these 3
things into my head? Absolutely!

1 Save a minimum of 10% to 20% of every gross dollar
you make. You will never miss it. It becomes a good
habit and good habits are hard to come by. Over time it
will be automatic.

2 Never finance a depreciating asset. Vehicles, RV's,
furniture, boats, you get the picture. It is easy to find
$500 or $1,000 cars that you can buy.   Save up and get that
"new" car down the road. Or never for that matter. They
are expensive and junky as far as I am concerned. These
days saving or coming up with $500 or $1,000 is easy.
Everyone has a car or two or three and lots of times they
just get rid of them. They are all over the place.

3 Never get a 30-year mortgage. A 30-year mortgage is
like taking your money out every month and burning
it in the driveway. Only get a 15-year mortgage. 10-year if
you can make it work. If you can afford and qualify for a
30-year mortgage you certainly can position your situation
in a reasonable amount of time and qualify for a 15-year
mortgage. No car payment and no credit card payments/
debt will make up the difference between the 2.

We all end up in one of a couple of the same places. Lying
on our backs looking straight up forever. Sitting in a wall in a
small urn. Or our ashes scattered some place of our choosing.

What astounds me constantly is most people work all day, work all week and work all month and then when it comes time to take care of the financial obligations they sit down and give all the money they earned to somebody else. They don't even give any of the money to themselves.

They work month after month, year after year for a life time. What they have left they go out and spend eating out, playing or just wasting it and hardly make it until it is time to get paid again. It is said, 78% of the working folks live pay check to pay check. It is a "life style" that is not easily broken. But it can be broken with some careful planning and executing that "Life's Plan."

There are a few things I don't dwell on in the following pages. Sex, religion, politics, your sexual preference and for sure your attitude. Where you are on those aspects of your life makes no difference to me. What does make a difference to me is enough of us in this country get to the point we don't let things go in the wrong direction for too long. That means enough of us must have a "Life's Plan" to make all this work.

If you disagree with what I have to say in the "101 Ways," think what I have said is foolish or stupid, doesn't make any sense, way off base, no way, you have got to be kidding, this guy is nuts, unstable isn't the word, please with all due respect keep one thing in mind:

Along with hoping you get an opportunity to join me in perfecting the "Art of Telling the World to Kiss Your Ass," you can kiss mine.

CHAPTER ONE

1. NOTHING LASTS FOREVER

As I look back over the last 65 plus years, there is one thing that I remember my Dad telling me after I moved to Alaska with my first wife Cheryl and our 2nd son Cameron. We were all making big money. The Pipe Line Days were booming. Anchorage, AK was booming. It was $100 bill times.

My Dad said. "David, you need to remember something: "nothing lasts forever."

He was right.

Now there are people that continue to buck that "nothing lasts forever" thinking. They get married and stay married. They are good stable fathers, mothers, husbands and wives. They buy a house, live in it long enough to pay it off, have a great career doing the same thing, save for retirement, live a structured and financially secure life. Some start a business and it is successful. Work the same job and retire with a good nest egg and a good pension. Good for them. They are not the norm, nor does it happen more than it doesn't happen.

There are an awful lot of "baby boomers" struggling now that they have gotten older. There are going to be even more of the next generation struggling because all they know how to do is turn on their iPhone.

Majority of the American working folks are having a very hard time making ends meet. Continuing to live a quality lifestyle just isn't going to happen when it comes time to retire. They don't have a clue how to keep physically and mentally healthy, emotionally perfected and financially sound. Why is this?

They never had a "Life's Plan."

They didn't save any money. They financed everything they did throughout their entire lives. They had 30-year mortgages instead of 15 or 10-year mortgages. Every dime they made they gave to somebody else. They were never in position cash wise to take an advantage of a down turn. They probably bought high and sold low or had to give it up during the hard times. They ate out all the time and spent the 20% they should have been saving at McDonalds or Chucky Cheese. They always drove two new cars, one a truck and one a SUV and financed them. Endless cell phones, Direct TV, credit cards, Macy's, Nordstrom. The buy now pays later mentality.

I know this wasn't and isn't everyone. I know a lot of folks my age who are "well off." But overall, as mentioned, 78% of the working-class people in this country live pay check to pay check. That is a fact and it won't unfortunately change. If you are young and just getting started and you don't "GET THIS" then you are going to struggle all your life. That is of course unless you win the lottery, or your parents leave you a substantial estate at an early age or you "marry" money.

So, listen up, keep an open mind, think about it and I guarantee you if you take the time to get serious and make a "Life's Plan" you won't regret it. If you don't, you will be 30, then 40, then 50, then 60, then 70. Then you will look back and wonder where all the years went and for sure wonder where in the hell did all that money go?

The answer is very simple: You gave it to somebody else!

CHAPTER TWO: PERSONAL

2. MAKE A "LIFE'S PLAN" JUST LIKE A BUSINESS PLAN.

The only business I have owned, out of several that were very successful initially was one that I had done a very detailed business plan for, before my wife Debbie and I started it. The first two years the business plan covered were phenomenally successful and went according to the plan. Then I/we got busy and I never updated the Business Plan to accommodate the rapid growth in the business itself and the changing environment of the customer and business environment. That was a huge mistake. Costs, growth and just about everything went south. That business didn't fail just because of that one reason, but it was in my opinion 20 years later the overriding reason.

Your life is no different than a business. Every business must or should have a business plan to navigate the unbelievable challenges in starting and growing a business. A life, your life is no different. It changes constantly. How can you get to where you are going if you don't have a road map? I don't know of anyone that starts out on a vacation for two weeks that doesn't have a good idea where they are going and what roads they are going to take to drive there. Let alone how much it is going to cost. That would be the same with getting on a plane and taking a vacation or going on a business trip. Virtually no one just goes to the airport and buys a ticket to "somewhere" and expects to make the all-important sales meeting with a million-dollar customer the next day. They buy a specific ticket, on a specific airline, going to that specific city, arriving in time to make the meeting. Along with where they are going to stay and how they are going to get to the meeting.

Life should be treated the same. If one sits down and starts to keep a journal for up to one year articulating their thoughts on what their personal goals are, what they want out of life, what their expectations are, where they see themselves in 5, 10, 15, 20, 25, 30 plus years down the road, this journal would be the outline for the "Life's Plan."

The most important thing is to keep track of where you spend your money daily. The only way this will be beneficial, and work is you are honest with yourself. At the end of that one year or sooner you should be able to put together your "Life's Plan" that will include and accommodate all those thoughts out of that journal. The same goes for married couples. Way too many married couples get married and 40 years goes by and they look back and can't believe how quick it went. Or another 20 years goes by with the 2nd marriage, but the results are the same.

Here is a list of 12 things that a study that older folks say they wish they would have been able to accomplish. These make sense to me and resonate with me. There are probably a 100 more of them.

1. Not being able to support their kids properly.

2. Not being able to put their kids thru college.

3. No having enough to retire comfortably, or at all.

4. Not investing in a business.

5. Not being able to purchase a second home.

6. Not being able to support their aging parents.

7. Not investing in the stock market.

8. Never seeming to have enough money.

9. Not having enough money for college, themselves.

10. Never starting a business.

11. Never taking a big trip.

12. Not being able to buy a house.

This isn't about regrets in my opinion. This is about making the choices and decisions early on in life. You won't end up with a list like the one above. Because you had a blue print to go by and a map to take you where you decided early on you wanted to be and you ended up where you planned on. A "Life's Plan" will make this happen.

It is a lot easier to live by a "Life's Plan" once it becomes a habit, a good habit at that. Living without a plan is very difficult, stressful and creates all kinds of challenges. In fact, it is chaotic. But it is absolutely guaranteed that if you create a "Life's Plan" and you follow it you will end up where you want to be. Living a very stress-free life, full of accomplishments and the fulfillment of goals is where the main goal out to be.

Try this. Periodically just go in the bathroom, or some place that is quiet and no one present. The bathroom is a great place. Sit down and just ask yourself. Am I happy with where I am in life? What is the problem? Chances are the answer to that question is, the problem is you. Stand up, look in the mirror and ask yourself.

Is there more that I can be doing? If you haven't started your "Life's Plan" then the answer to that is, yes, there is a lot more you can and should be doing. For yourself as well as your family if you have one or are about to have one.

3. KNOW WHERE YOU HAVE BEEN, WHERE YOU ARE AND WHERE YOU ARE GOING.

When was the last time you got in your car drove someplace, turned around and drove back to where you started? That could be to the store, to work, to visit some friends or go to a movie. Simple right? The next day you had no idea where you went yesterday on that drive, nor did you know how you got back or where you were going next. That never happens unless you get Dementia or Alzheimer's over night. But this is exactly how most young people and even people later in life live their lives. They don't have a clue.

The only way you can learn anything is to experience it, learn it thru studying it or having someone lay it out for you. A "Life's Plan" lays it out for you. We all need to grow up some time. I never even had a clue until I got sober at 50. Then it took another 3 years to realize how dysfunctional I had been all those years. I thought I was normal and functioning as an adult. It was far from it.

Some of us get it functioning as an adult early on in life, others it takes a life time. Some never get it. But knowing where you have been with your life's experiences and understanding the consequences or benefits of those experiences is crucial early on. No matter how limited they may be at an early age, a "Life's Plan" allows you to leap into the world of responsibility. There is nothing more rewarding than setting a personal goal and achieving it. It becomes a "good" habit. It becomes easier to do as we set more goals and achieve them.

Without goals in life and knowing exactly how you are going to conduct your life daily you got problems coming. Having a "Life's Plan" will immediately create a living experience that will create benefits and rewards way beyond your imagination.

4. GET IN CONTROL OF YOUR LIFE.

Each one of us at some point in our lives spins out of control. It shows up in a 2-year old's tantrum at the grocery store because he can't have what he wants. Or it shows up when our truck breaks down at 40 years old, it is Christmas and we are alone and a relationship we believed in didn't work. It builds up and the dam finally breaks.

The "Life's Plan" can help deal with these types of challenges. Once we get on our own, it shouldn't take long to realize we need escape mechanisms to overcome the constant barrage of challenges that life throws at us. Life today is tough. That is just a fact. The pressures of succeeding, family, friends, financial and social expectations can create a tremendous amount of stress and anxiety. In that "Life's Plan" there must be a chapter/section on how to cope with challenges as they are presented.

Get in control of your life by creating things to do when this stress and anxiety becomes overwhelming. Each one of us will come up with different and similar things to do to take control. Realizing what works for you and what doesn't is critical to maintaining a healthy mental and emotional balance when things go sideways.

All sound business plans have what it takes to be successful. But few good business plans have an exit plan if things don't work out and the business needs to be shut down. A busi-

ness can be shut down way before it is time to file bankruptcy or the business goes broke.

Your "Life's Plan" should also have an exit plan. You should
have "an exit plan on how to exit a working life" and transition into retirement. Your plan should also give you specific ways to control the stress and the anxiety that is sure to
happen at some point in time.

It can be a variety of things. Going for a run or a walk,
doing meditation or yoga, going for a long hike or camping
trip to get grounded and centered again. Staying in a state
of stress and anxiety is not healthy. We all know it. But few
of us have ways to cope with it when it hits.

5. SUSPECT ANYTHING AND EVERYTHING.

I pretty much have gotten to the point that I don't believe anything I read that comes from the internet. It has been years and years since I read newspapers to try to keep up with what is going on in the world. It has also been years since I have watched TV. If you repeat something that you have read on the internet, read in the newspapers or hear/see it on TV and you believe it to be true your nuts.

Not that the ridiculousness didn't go on before things got to the point they have, but it is so bad now, one article says it is black and another article right below it on Yahoo says it is white. News isn't news anymore. It is all bullshit and it is not going to get any better.

So, when it comes to making decisions, one must really seek out the facts, make decisions based upon personal experiences and the experiences of those you trust. Then make the decision and execute.

The idea that you can plan certain aspects of your life around what you get off the internet, from the newspapers and TV these days is going to do nothing but create problems in your life.

It is sad, but I really don't trust anything or anybody any more but those in my sphere of influence.

6. MAKE UP YOUR OWN MIND ON EVERYTHING.

Making up your own mind on pretty much everything you plan on doing is where you will end up making the right decisions. I am not saying that you should go "blind" into the night. But with good intelligence and seeking out the facts and knowing right from wrong in your own gut, will almost always lead to the right decisions.

I can't imagine calling up somebody I barely know, or don't know at all and ask them should I do this, or should I do that? It has got to the point for me that I make all my own decisions without really consulting anybody. Good or bad, it has and continues to work for me. The positive results of this I believe bear out when it comes to my health. I have been pushed several times in my life to get on one medication or another and I have refused.

A gut feeling normally will lead one in the right directions and you will end up making the right decisions. Now I am not trying to suggest that you should try performing brain surgery on your best friend because your gut tells you it is the right thing to do. I am saying that we all have built into our being, our souls a keen sense of direction and where right versus wrong is.

My long kayak trip is on the Yukon River, a 1,600 mile plus trip took a good deal of research. I read blogs, journals and books of those that have done this trip before me. I have traversed the river numerous times on Google Earth. But the fact is, this trip on the Yukon will was no different than the rest of the trips I have taken. With the right gear and my experience, I don't need somebody to tell me what to do or how to do it, nor will I ask. Nor do I need to ask anybody how I get there and how I get back. The decisions I have made preparing for this trip were no different than all the decisions you need to make on anything.

Common sense, seeking out those that has experienced it before and you yourself are more than enough to make a sound decision.

7. WATCHING TV IS A WASTE OF TIME.

I don't mean to be insulting to anybody.

You want to get stupid, or stupider? Then watch TV every day. I can't think of anything that is more insulting than what the boob tube has on it these days. You talk about degrading and outright disrespectful. It absolutely flabbergasts me that anybody would spend 2 seconds watching TV. That goes for the news, let alone the reality shows, the game shows, the sitcoms and movies all the time.

Every time I do get put into a situation where the TV is on it is the same thing as it was 10 years ago. Nothing has changed.

I believe it affects your emotional, physical and your financial health to sit night after night or day after day as a lot of people do and watch TV. What is wrong with you if you do? Just think of all the things you could be doing if you weren't sitting on your ass watching TV.

It doesn't take any brains at all or be a genius to realize that the best thing you could do for yourself and your family is throwing that damn thing away. Sell it or give it away.

I know people use it for "entertainment" or a diversion to reality.

A lot of people use it to fill in time, especially in the evening. Slumping on a couch, drinking beer and watching TV is a very poor substitute for genuine relaxation.

There are so many other things one can be doing that are productive, healthy, entertaining, worthwhile and rewarding.

In no way do I mean to be disrespectful to anybody, but it makes no sense to me. Some people have a half dozen TV's in their house and all of them are on at the same time.

This day and age it's bad enough with the smart phones and the social media. You throw the TV in with these two things and we have an entire generation that has grown up "stupid" and completely "worthless." I won't be around in the next 50 years to witness the repercussions of this "stupidity", but I have a feeling it won't be pretty.

8. READING THE NEWSPAPER IS A WASTE OF TIME.

Here we go again. What a waste of time and demoralizing. Anybody with an IQ over 5 should realize, in my opinion, that newsprint today is nothing more than a bunch of ideal-ists trying to convince you they know what is going on and what is good for you.

You are better off to exercise, go for a walk, read a book or just listen to the birds singing than you are to sit down and read a newspaper.

9. DON'T DO ANYTHING YOU DON'T WANT TO.

When I got sober over 20 years ago one of things I did was make a "deal" with myself. I decided that I wasn't going to do anything I didn't want to. Now, that deal didn't include going to the dentist because I didn't want to. Nor did it include not taking the garbage out. Or cleaning the house. Or washing the windows. Or paying the bills.

What it did include was when situations arise that make me feel uncomfortable or I know what the outcome is going to be which won't be in my favor, I don't do it. I don't go there. I don't participate. I don't buy it. I don't talk about it. I don't eat it.

I don't. I don't. I don't.

We all must do a lot of things we don't want to. But I submit to you, that if you work at getting "Free" by working your "Life's Plan," executing that plan and working hard at getting to where that plan is taking you. Then at some point in time, sooner than later, you will never have to do anything you don't want to.

The difference in my life today, then when I was unaware of the fact I had choices in my life is amazing. I don't have many bad days. Nor do I have many bad hours. This is because I choose to stay focused on what works for me. Not what somebody else wants or expects of me.

I have learned to not spend any time at all worrying about why I made the amount of wrong choices I have in the past. Instead, I spend my valuable time on making sure I make the right choices for the future.

10. DO NOT LET PEOPLE TAKE AN ADVANTAGE OF YOU.

Here is what I mean by "don't let people take an advantage of you." I am not particularly referring to physically taking an advantage of you, but rather emotionally. People can play word games, say things that hurt you, upset you, make things miserable for you, put you off, get you to thinking, worrying, stressing and more importantly causes you to react in negative ways.

More importantly, they can get you to spend your money, what little bit you have.

By hitting these hot buttons, they are taking an advantage of you for their own satisfaction. We all do it. All the time. But by having a "Life's Plan" that includes ways to not set yourself up or get set up, it can almost eliminate situations where you are going to be taken an advantage of.

There are also ways people can take an advantage of you from a financial perspective. If you have a budget that you live by, swear by and refuse to deviate from, this is probably the best defense you could ever have to not getting yourself into situations to let people take an advantage of you. If you do happen to be in a "sound financial" position, family, friends, work associates and business associates are going to "ask for money." It is inevitable. I guarantee you if you have the "Life's Plan" and you are living by it, you will get into a "sound financial" position sooner than later.

11. LOOK OUT, IF YOU JUST SAID "YES."

#11 and the next one #12 from my life's experiences are two of the most important "Ways."

Each one of us can remember instances where we wished we would have just said "No." "Yes" creates all kinds of opportunities for a whole lot of grieve and heartache, let alone risk and no rewards. There are a lot of folks that wish they would have never said "Yes" to a request to go, to participate, to loan money, to get married, to start a partnership, to spend time, to spend money on this or that, to go to dinner, to go to the show, to start a business, or just leave the house.

Now I am not advocating that you live in a world where you do nothing. But taking the time to analyze the request for an answer of yes or no, can eliminate a lot of potential grieve.

The same goes for "questioning" what your answer out to be. A whole lot of people didn't make it home last night and their last stop in life was the mortuary, only because they said yes rather than no. They didn't spend one second thinking about what their answer should have been.

Just think about this and give it more than a passing thought. Can you tell me a more significant and sound way of "Telling the World to Kiss Your Ass" than being in 100% control of your life and your own destiny that your thought process gives you the luxury to say "NO" and mean it.

12. LEARN TO SAY NO.

You don't have to be a jerk or negative individual to say "No." I suppose one could come up with some consequences of saying "NO" at the wrong time or to a request. From my experiences, answering "No" eliminates a whole lot more potential consequence in life than "Yes."

This day and age just going to the mall can be a wrong decision. Leaving home 4 times a day to go do the chores is a whole lot riskier than making a list and just leaving once a day to accomplish your daily chores.

Driving while intoxicated or impaired of course "isn't like it was in my glorious days." I am not proud of it, but I have had 9 DUI's. Every single one of those DUI's could have easily been prevented if I just would have answered the question I asked each time of myself, should I drive or not? A simple "No" would have changed the course of my life from negative to positive many, many times over.

Loaning money is another big No. I am not saying you can't help someone out when the need arises under common sense parameters. However, I have given a lot of money away. I have never made a loan. If you give it away as a gift, then the expectation of it being paid back is not part of the decision to do so.

It just boils down to the simple fact, that currently there are all kinds of "risks" one takes in just leaving the house to do anything. You must analyze and determine if the rewards of making a decision that involves Yes, outweighs the risks involved.

I know I am strange. I know what I think most of the time is out of the norm. But I don't put myself in many situations where a terrorist or a mad man is going to toss a grenade in my car. They normally don't waste grenades on one individual.

When I am driving, I drive defensively, never offensively or aggressively. You always have the right away with me, I'll never get right on your bumper, nor will I ever "flip you off". You will just see me smile at you. Give you a pleasant nod while under my breath I am "telling you to kiss my ass."

This probably is going to be one of the most ridiculously things some people will think I have put down in writing in this little book. I know very well what the word "addiction" means. But I just for the life of me can't fathom why people drink to excess with so many avenues these days to get help, an alcoholic or not. I still don't understand the drugs or this overdosing on prescription medications. One of the things that astounds me is how a lot of people get obese, let alone fat. I fully realize some of this over weightiness is hereditary, but most of it is just plain eating too much and way too much of the wrong foods and for sure sitting around watching the TV, on the I-Phone, playing computer games and no physical activity.

The sooner you learn to say "No" the better your life is going to be.

13. DO WHAT YOU WANT.

Sounds simple and it is. Why would you do something you don't want to do? This is just the opposite of "Don't Do Anything You Don't Want to Do." This is just a matter of some life's experiences and common sense. A lot of people have trouble finding their way on this. I am trying to make this more of "following" the "Life's Plan" than I am suggesting that you should smoke a pound of dope every day, because that is what you want to do. There are a lot of things we would like to do, but we don't because of all the right reasons.

You need to learn to do the right things. Make the right things a habit, not a burdensome chore. Saving money is a big one. Once you have taken the time to keep track of how you spend your money, I guarantee you when it is time to start executing your "Life's Plan" and live by your budget, you will consistently be doing what you want to do.

14. GO WHERE YOU WANT.

Some of these "101 Ways" might seem redundant, and perhaps they are. But that is what life is to a degree, redundancy. It is consistently doing the same thing day in and day out. Unfortunately, way too many of us do the wrong things consistently day in and day out.

One of the worst things I did when I was young, just married and starting a family was stop at the tavern to drink beer and BS with the boys. It was the beginning of a lot of bad habits for a very long time.

Where the biggest rewards in life come from is in doing the "right things" day in and day out. Stopping at the tavern for a beer with the boys is not one of those right things. Doesn't sound like much but is was a huge mistake on my part and was the beginning of a lot of bad habits that I did consistently day in and day out.

Exercising your will to create good habits thru your "Life's Plan" will give you the opportunity do and go where you want. More importantly it puts you closer and closer to being able to "Tell the World to Kiss Your Ass."

It is all part of the plan. It is my opinion, based upon a lot of experience; each one of us can pretty much do or go where ever we want to. We just need to figure out what it is going to take, make the plan and then work towards accomplishing it. It is purely by the numbers. It can be as simple as a weekend camping trip or a trip around the world. Or it can be a million dollars in the bank. It is all relative and becomes part of the plan.

It all has to do with time and money. Communicating with yourself and others is also a big part of achieving your goals. Managing it all with careful planning is all it takes. Religiously adhering to the goals set out in the "Life's Plan" you will be very amazed at how soon your have put yourself into a position to execute the weekend camping trip or the trip around the world, or a bank account that allows you to get "Free."

15. HAVE SEVERAL HOBBIES.

Sorry, but I don't consider watching TV, DVD Movies, the I Phone, playing computer games or any other such thing as a hobby.

Here is what takes place in my life pretty much daily. I eat very well. I practice the Native Flute, I listen and watch Piano Practicing Videos (about ready to buy a piano). I always have a project going on, right now rebuilding a 1929 1 ½ ton Chevy with an old Prairie Schooner type camper on the back. Also refinishing a 1952 Klepper kayak. Just finishing up a small remodel for the Attorney for the Native American Tribe on the reservation I am staying. I also kayak/paddle a lot. I read in the evenings and listen to good piano or relaxing music almost nightly.

I take a walk for at least four plus miles every day and exercise after that walk. I just made a large Elk Horn Chandelier for my next tipi, building and putting graphics on seven small tipi lamp shades. This is what I mean by having some hobbies. I started painting several months ago and enjoy it greatly.

The most important thing about doing multiple things is you are preparing yourself for retirement. Way too many people are retiring without any hobbies or anything to do and they end up fat from sitting around watching TV, smoke way too much, eat way too much, drink way too much and drop dead.

With the hobbies as a part of your "Life's Plan" then it has become another one of those good habits that you have been doing for years.

There is no way you are ever going to get into a position "To Tell the World to Kiss Your Ass" if you don't get in control.

If you don't find a way to stay busy, keep healthy both mentally and physically you are doomed.

16. LOOK FOR WAYS TO HELP OTHERS.

This is probably one of the best ways to stay healthy both emotionally and physically. Helping somebody else in need is such a rewarding way to relieve stress and anxiety and it also puts a perspective on just how fortunate one is, in so many ways.

I have never been good at this. But I do give a ton of money away to the folks standing on the corner. Guess that is my way of "helping somebody else." But I am always trying to hold the door open for somebody behind me, always looking for somebody to say a kind word to.

To be sure, if I stayed in one place long enough, I would be volunteering some place on a continual basis to help where I could do the most good with my life's experiences.

There are many ways we can all help those in need or those that are less fortunate. The return for the investment in time is way beyond imagination if you haven't done enough to get that feeling.

This is another one of those ways to get in control of your life. Doing for others and living up to that commitment, gets you that much closer to the big "Bend Over."

17. ABOVE ALL ELSE, BE YOURSELF.

Unfortunately, this is not easy to do these days. I know and have known a lot of folks who try to pretend that they are what they aren't. Being yourself, finding your own values and depth of character is one of the most important ways of "being yourself."

Why is being you so important? I have always said that I constantly have 3 guys supporting me. There is me, my soul and my spirit. I am never alone. Over the years there have been many very lively discussions about what course to take amongst these three guys, or what decision to make or what direction to go in.

But if I am true to myself, using the wisdom and knowledge that has been gleaned from the past, the right decision is always made. That hasn't been as often as it should have been. There is nothing wrong with seeking out comments, advice and suggestions. But the fact is only you and you alone have the depth of wisdom and experience to make that all-important decision.

It is when the ego gets involved that one can get into trouble. Fame and fortune are most often the culprit and of course ego is right up there when it comes to trying to keep things in perspective. Doing what others expect of you from their perspective rather than your own is not a healthy avenue to take.

Being true to one's self is once again one of those functions in life that can contribute to getting to the point of being "Free" that you are seeking. It is also another one of those good habits that I belief doesn't come so naturally.

Being true to one's self is essential to leading a life in control. It must be a learned function in life to be able to get you closer and closer to perfecting your "Life's Plan," hence giving you a better chance:

"To Tell the World to Kiss Your Ass."

18. IF YOU NEED ADVICE; SEEK IT, AND THEN ADVISE YOURSELF.

Life is full of decisions. It doesn't matter what day it is, we all have dozens and dozens of decisions to make. Most of these decisions on how we are going to approach something or how we are going to do this and that are made early in life and that is the way we do things day in and day out. The routine we set for ourselves in the morning remains the same. How we comb our hair, how we brush our teeth, how we go about the business of the day, the route we take to work and back home. How we dress and what we eat. It all pretty much remains the same throughout our entire lives.

What I am referring to on seeking advice and then advising yourself has more to do with the "life altering" decisions such as: What college do I go to? Should I join the service before going to college? What career path should I choose? Should I take this job or not? Should I marry this man or woman? Should I use drugs or not? Should I buy this car or not? Should we buy a house or keep renting? What town do we live in or even what part of the country do we live in? These types of decisions can be what leads down a path of self destruction or just the opposite, leads you down a path of success and joy.

I personally think a lot of people have a self destruct side to them. They possess a fear of being successful, which con-stantly pushes them into making bad decisions. Most of the time, giving into a bad decision is a lot easier than making a good decision.

Bad habits are easy, good habits are hard.

Asking your parents, your friends, your work associates, your spouse, your girlfriend, boyfriend or significant other if you should do this or that is what most of us do and should.

Even going to the internet is big thing today to get the answer. However, when it comes to making the right decision, the best decision, that decision should come from you. Doesn't mean it can't be the same as what most of your advice is.

I once heard a guy say that was getting his 20 year AA chip how did he stay sober all these years. His response was, "I always make a decision that doesn't go against my guy feeling. If it doesn't feel right in my gut, then chances are it isn't right for me." Common sense should always be part of any decision. We all have it in us to know what is right for us. It is our soul and our spirit talking to us. You know. Now grant it, there are individuals that have mental issues that prevent them from knowing right and wrong, good from evil that makes them turn violent and end up in prison or dead.

One of the greatest feelings of satisfaction you can have is making a decision that is the right one. It all turns out as planned. It feels good. So, when it comes to seeking out advice, get it, lots of it. But make that decision that feels right.

Don't just convince yourself it is right. Feel it in your gut it is right. Then make the decision.

19. LEARN TO ENTERTAIN YOURSELF.

One of my claims to fame has been "I am not the entertainment director." This for sure never made my wife Debbie happy to hear me say it. For almost 28 years I never put forth much effort to "entertain" her, us or anyone else for that matter. That was and still is a character flaw on my part. Not particularly conducive to a sound flourishing relationship.

But, I am a big believer in "entertaining yourself." I don't need anybody to lead me into doing something, or be with me, or have coffee with me, which I don't drink, or go to the movie with me which I might go once a year, or river raft a river, or kayak a lake or river. I do fine by myself, thank you. I always have. This pattern of entertaining myself was set early on in life and has worked very well most of the time for me.

I am one of those people that needs a list. I need to know what I am doing, where I am going, what the reason for doing it is, what I need and when I am going to get it. I pretty much know what I am going to do daily, weekly, monthly and a couple of years down the road. I am constantly reviewing a daily financial budget, then weekly, then monthly and then yearly. I often plan out on paper, a list if you will, on what my plans are for the next two or three years. It isn't in cast in stone, but it gives me a "blue print"…a way of visualizing it. Doesn't mean it all has to happen. I believe it is part of the "Life's Plan" that I constantly change and adapt to with the changing way life is all the time.

As I have said, I don't watch TV. That gives me a lot of time to entertain myself. Having a variety of things to do I believe keeps me physically active, keeps my brain working and above all it keeps me motivated to get the best out of every day.

It also keeps me in control. Complete control. What better way could there possibly be to "Tell the World to Kiss Your Ass" than being in complete control?

20. NO ONE IS GOING TO TAKE CARE OF YOU WHEN THE TIME COMES BUT YOU.

Many of us have found out over the years, especially us older folks, that when it gets right down to it, no one is going to take care of you but you. Whether it is family, friends, business associates or strangers, no one is going to give you a call and ask you if they can make your mortgage payment or rent payment for you this coming month out of the goodness of their heart. Even if they can afford it and it is pocket change to them, it isn't going to happen.

When was the last time, unless it was your father for a graduation present said, "come on with me, we will go down and buy you a new car. I will pay cash, so you don't have a car payment and your insurance won't be much just on liability insurance and you don't have to pay me back.

Now to be sure, you can ask one of those members of your family, a friend, and a business associate or get a loan to make that mortgage or rent payment, buy that car, but it is going to cost you. Chances are if you can not make the payment, you won't get the money anyway. Housing, transportation and food are the 3 biggest expenditures that we make monthly out of our income. This total of expenditure amounts to approximately 62% plus or minus. That doesn't leave much left over.

When you are down and out for whatever reason, it is much harder to get help. When you are sailing high, everyone wants to help you and be a part of the glory. I believe this society we live in today, relishes the opportunity to kick someone when they are down.

Getting in control of your life, creating an ongoing situation where you will never need help from anyone, is one of the sure-fire ways to get into a position "To Tell the World to Kiss Your Ass."

You will never ever get into this position if you don't create a "Life's Plan" and stick to it and make it all happen through repetition and creating good habits. Just because everyone else spends 62% of what they have after taxes on housing, transportation and food doesn't mean you have to.

21. BE PREPARED FOR ANYTHING.

Once again some of these "Ways" may seem redundant. They are all independent of one another. Each one stands alone. You must practice getting in control of your own destiny. Being prepared for anything is one of the best ways to exercise control and stay in control.

Being prepared for anything includes never leaving the house without having some survival supplies in the trunk of your car or in you tool box in the back of your truck, even if it is for weekend trip.

Couple extra bucks stuck away some place certainly would make sense.

Folks living in tornado alley and along the East Coast know what it means to be prepared. Even when I am on a long kayak trip, I always have a bag that has survival things in it. Which means if I were to lose my kayak, somebody steals it, or I put a hole in it I can't fix, I have a day pack that I keep with me and I could survive for close to four to six days. Even in the worst of weather I would survive very well.

Being prepared for anything also means you must be prepared financially. A good six months of savings or cash in a coffee can solves that problem. Of course, if you didn't make a "Life's Plan" and haven't been executing it, chances are you don't have that six plus months savings or the cash available to attack a problem that comes up. It can be a multitude of things. Being prepared is essential.

It also refers to being prepared emotionally. People die. Dogs get hit by cars. Cats get run over. Parents get old and pass away and for sure friendships wither and disappear. Relationships ending with a significant other are one of the hardest things any of us must go through. If we aren't prepared to deal with it, we can fall off the deep end very quickly. Keeping healthy physically, strong emotionally and aware of reality are the best ways to be prepared. Oh, and having a few bucks helps also.

Your "Life's Plan" should have a section in it that covers this part of your life as time goes by. That section on how to prepare you for anything will ultimately end up covering several of the 101 Ways.

22. PREPARE FOR THE FUTURE

If you are young and just starting this path to "Freedom",
then you are going to need to gather all the...been there
and done that you can. You need to get all the information
you can from others that have gone before you, experienced
successes and failures.

One could spend a life time seeking out information thru
reading a multitude of books that clearly explain and shows
you a path to financial, emotional and mental success. Few
read them, less comprehend them and not many put the
experience of others into practice.

With the access to the vast amounts of information on the
internet, multitude of books written, older family members,
relatives, friends, associates and your own experiences in life,
there is no reason, or excuse good enough to not get with
it. This isn't a plug for anybody or any mythology of getting
"Free" and finding happiness. But if you aren't following
Dave Ramsey's method to achieve your freedom and financial success then you are missing something very important.

Far too many of today's younger generation spend much
of their time with their face in the phone. It never fails to
amaze me that even in the airport, 99% of the people have
their phone in their hand and all they do is play with it.
Sad, disrespectful, stupid, waste of time and more importantly this country has and continues to lose an entire generation to the social media and smart phone debacle.

In my humble opinion, Steve Jobs and that Facebook guy didn't do this country or any other country for that matter any favors.

The future is here every day at midnight. The older you get, the faster it goes by. The more you do, the faster it goes by. The more money you make, the faster it goes by. Before long, you are having your 68th birthday and it is too late. What you want to have happen is look back a couple of weeks after your 55th birthday or sooner, your retired, at least 1 million in the bank, drawing interest you can live on and constantly looking around and telling everyone and the world "To Kiss Your Ass."

Decide, get prepared, start working on that "Life's Plan" and start keeping track of where all your hard-earned money is going every day. Keep of list of your bad habits and the few good habits you probably have.

Get rid of the bad habits.

23. LISTEN TO YOUR SOUL AND YOUR SPIRIT.

People have always wondered how I can spend so much time alone. I am never alone. There is always someone with me. There is me, my soul and my spirit. It certainly makes for some lively discussions at times. Never does one of us have a complete say in things.

Then there is always that little guy that resides in my gut. He constantly is making trouble. We all know what right and what wrong is. It is instilled in us from the beginning of life, probably before we are born.

I read a blog the other day a lady called them "monkeys" running around in her head. At times it feels like I have a half a dozen of those monkeys causing problems.

We know there are individuals that have a mind that doesn't know right from wrong. There are institutions and prisons full of them. There are obviously a lot of folks in prison that do know right from wrong and they made the wrong decision.

But for us normal folk, we have hundreds of decisions to make day in and day out. What matters every single day is each decision we make is the right one and not the wrong one.

Listen to your soul and or your spirit or both. Your gut feelings normally will push you in the right decision.

Lot of decisions are instantaneous. They just happen. We don't even think about them. Work at making sure they are the right ones.

What I am referring to is when it comes to the "Life's Plan," making the decisions to get serious about your life and your future are an individual thing. It is simple. It is easy. The results are immediate and rewarding. There are consequences for bad decisions and bad habits. There are rewards for good decisions and good habits. Good habits are just that, they are good for you.

Why is that so hard for a lot of us to grasp?

You want to get "Free"? You want to be in control? You want to get debt free? You want to get into a position to do exactly as you want to? Then quit being a stugoofid. Get with it. Start keeping track of what is going on in your life and start to make that outline for your "Life's Plan."

A good start is shut your phone down in the evenings for 3 hours. I know you have already got rid of the TV.

24. GET SPIRITUAL.

This is not talking about going to church, kissing a rattle-snake or wearing a beanie. It also isn't talking about getting baptized, becoming a priest or an altar boy. These things are fine and dandy but there is more. I grew up as a Christian Scientist. My mother was one and remained one all her life. Later in mid life, I was baptized in the Baptist Church.

When I left for Vietnam I was scared so I started reading the bible. Don't know if that is what saved my ass or not, but it did give me a sense of calm sometimes. I carried a small bible with me the entire time I was in Vietnam. I figured it couldn't hurt, but if I remember correctly I spent more time figuring out how to get 4 or 6 beers a day during resupply than the allotted 2 than trying to see if God was protecting me. I certainly asked him to when the bullets were flying.

What this refers to is finding that "high power" that gives you an edge. We all have one and if you don't know what yours is, you need to figure it out. Even an "atheist" finds a way to work thru things, relying on something to get thru the thick of it.

Finding the right balance in life, staying centered and grounded is an art. It doesn't just happen. There are way too many curve balls thrown at us constantly. That if we don't have that "rock" to lean on, some of us can get into trouble very quickly.

For me my "spirituality" comes from nature. The sun, the moon, the trees, the birds singing, the wildlife, the animals, the water, the fish jumping, the eagles talking, the beaver's tail hitting the water, the Osprey fishing, the swallows skimming the water, the crows talking, the chukars clucking, the deer blowing at night and the coyotes howling. You get the picture.

When I go for walks, which is never down main street, I know where my spirituality is if things are right in my life, because I feel like I am walking on air. When I am out of sync, ungrounded, wobbling around like a top, I know my spirituality is out of whack and my priority becomes finding out why. Immediately.

No way will you ever get to the "Big Bend Over" if you don't have a good spiritual grounding.

25. HAVE A SENSE OF HUMOR.

This part of the process of getting "Free" is probably just about as important as anything. Way too many of us take ourselves and life way to seriously. There are also way too many people in this world who think they are the center of the universe. What it all boils down to no matter who we are, how much money we have, how much we are seen in the movies, on the TV or on the front page of the newspapers across this country, none of us amounts to nothing more than a speck of fly shit on an elephant's butt.

When the time comes for you to take your last breath, nothing is going to give you the next one. Nothing. I would rather go out with a smile on my face, sober, with having had a good laugh recently than bitter, pissed off, angry and resentful. Now I know when that last breath comes for a lot of us, we have no control

During the journey down the road, why not as often as you can have a smile on your face, a laugh several times a day and enjoy the trip? There is always going to be dead batteries and flat tires. Then there is the boyfriend you daughter brings home and the only thing you say to yourself is "boy ain't he pretty." People get fired from their job or didn't get that job. Cars break down, electricity is cut off, businesses fails, the check didn't show up in the mail, the list is endless. When you get right down to it, I don't care what it has been in my life I thought was a huge deal at the time, 10, 15, 20 years down the road it just didn't make any difference.

I am not talking about the kind of laughing and fun you supposedly can get out of a reality show or from a sitcom on TV. I am talking about the kind of fun and laughter you can enjoy and get out of experiences and relationships.

My sense of humor runs deep and has always been a little bit off the wall. But it is one of those more important aspects of my life that helps keep me grounded and centered.

The most important part of having a sense of humor is not taking yourself too seriously and being able to laugh at your mistakes and faults.

It will be virtually impossible for you to ever be "Free" without a sense of humor.

26. YOU DON'T USUALLY CHANGE WHO YOU ARE BECAUSE YOU WANT TO.   YOU CHANGE WHO YOU ARE BECAUSE YOU HAVE TO.

We folks who are a little bit older can probably relate to #26 more than the younger guys and gals. When we take the time to understand who we are, what are best attributes are and what are true character defects are, is when we start to figure out what we need to change.

It can come from drinking too much.   Using too many drugs prescribed or off the street. Eating too much and being overweight. Knowing in our gut and heart we should be nicer to the spouse or the kids. Being a better husband and father is at the top of any list. Trying to be a better employee or boss is a big one. Driving slower or faster, exercising, riding a bike, running, or walking eating this or not eating that and going here or going there. Bad relationships are a big one. Too much TV is at the top of the list.   This list can also be endless. It can just go on and on and on.

We normally aren't too old before we know what we need to change or add to or take away from our lives to become a better person. OK, a better person is nice, but how about becoming not only a better person but a "Free" one at that.

I am not proud of this whenever I tell the story, but after I got my 9th DUI, it took me another six months to quit drinking. How could that be? The only answer I can come up with after 20 plus years of sobriety is I was one very sick, stressed out, confused, unbalanced and for sure a little crazy individual. But once I got it, I got it good. I never looked back, and I would take a bullet before I ever drank again.

If there was ever a case where "you don't usually change who you are because you want to, you change who you are because you have to" it was me. It was either change or die.

It didn't take me long to figure out after a tremendous amount of counseling thru the VA and attending AA Meetings that no question I had issues. I was not the normal individual/man I thought I was. Far from it.

I changed. Big time. I am not the same person I was for the 1st 50 years of my life. I have no desire to go back to who I was during that time. What a waste of a life. But I am making up for it as best as I can.

Happy, Joyous and Free is my goal. I pursue it with a passion each day. Don't think for a minute that I don't look around me and wonder what is taking so and so....so long to figure this out. I never lecture, never sound off or present myself as holier than thou. But I do strive to set an example in my small world of influence and hope it gets noticed.

I can remember my mother telling me as a young boy "that there is a huge difference in thinking you are good and knowing you are good." Thinking you are good is your ego leading the way. Knowing you are good is having confidence in yourself and proving it.

This must be one of the best ways to get to the point of proving to the world that when you "Tell the World to Kiss Your Ass" you can…. because you are "Free" in every way.

27. HAPPINESS IS SOMEWHERE BETWEEN TOO MUCH AND NOT ENOUGH.

Being broke, sick, destitute, can't make ends meet, alone, car is not running, and you don't have the money to fix it, your wife or girl friend or significant other ran off with the UPS driver yesterday and you lost your wallet. These situations don't make for a whole lot of happiness. But we all experience them.

Some of us go rob a bank. Others go deeper into debt. A few get drunk, get a DUI or OD on drugs. Some go get a job or even a second job and somehow make it all work out at the end of the month.

On the other side of the fence, you have several million dollars in the bank. Live in a million-dollar home that is paid for. You own free and clear all three of your $80,000 vehicles. The plane has plenty of hours left on it before it needs attention and your boat is waiting at the harbor with its crew ready to take you and yours to the Bahamas. Couldn't get any better, right? But two days before you leave for some unknown reason you jump off the bridge, leaving a suicide note saying, "you just can't stand it anymore." This sort of thing happens all the time.

That spot somewhere in-between too much and not enough is hard to find. It is called happiness, contentment, grounded, centered, and aware of where you are in life. You are in contact with your higher power, in control of your spirituality. You know things are good and you are constantly striving to make things better. So where is it? When is enough, enough?

I can't answer that for you nor do I think anybody else can. I know, or at least I have a pretty good idea where it is for me.

It is when I don't want anything or need anything, and all my needs are being met.

Now the emotional side of this conversation can be a whole different set of circumstances and I am not pretending to have enough knowledge of that to articulate.

But I do know when it comes to setting up a "Life's Plan" and getting to the point of being able to "Tell the World to Kiss Your Ass" you need to make sure you are being honest with yourself about everything. What is it you want to achieve? How you are going to get there?

Having a whole lot of "crap" is not the way to make it happen. A sound relationship, good fiscal habits and knowing your limitations and capabilities will get you a long way to achieving your goal of getting "Free."

28. WHEN THE TIME COMES, THERE IS NO GETTING A 2ND CHANCE.

There are a lot of things we all do or attempt to do, and we fail. We don't quite achieve our goals. We decide to try again and some of us must keep trying and trying and trying. From my experiences having a plan to achieve those goals is a lot easier than just taking off blind.

What #28 means is when you are about to take your last breath, if you get lucky enough to last that long and don't get taken out early on in life, is that no matter how hard you pray or how many times you ask "Him" for just a little more time, it isn't going to happen.

So why not plan on making the best of the time you have? The time you have as you get older becomes less and less. Every minute, hour, day, week, month and year you waste fighting the battle and never winning just takes you that much closer to the end.

Think about it. The sooner you get "Free" the sooner you can enjoy life to the fullest, whatever that is for you. If you keep trying to keep up with your friends, make another $10,000 or if you are lucky another $100,000 can be fatal. Getting that new truck, you don't need or buying that bigger house that you don't walk into half of the rooms or take that next cruise and you didn't enjoy the last one, is reason to pause and evaluate just what is important in your life.

What is important to you? It is different for all of us.

Having that "Life's Plan" and executing it sooner than later is going to get you "Free." It is inevitable that it will happen. How many times have you bought something that needs to be put together? You struggle and struggle, but it just doesn't come together. You finally relent and pull the instructions out of the garbage. 10 minutes later it is together and operating or useable. Your "Life's Plan" is no different.

You will never get your life together and functioning at 100% if you don't plan it to happen that way.

Here are a couple of things that will help you get started. Get off the couch. Throw that F_____ TV away. Get off the F_____ phone. Get with it.

29. WHEN IS ENOUGH, ENOUGH?

What a great question. It goes to the heart of a lot of stress
and challenges these days that most people are carrying
around with them. It also goes right to the center of a lot of
problems couples have. When do you have enough spoons
in the kitchen drawer? More importantly it also goes to the
emotional/mental aspects of what we all are dealing with
these days. Information overload, social media bombard-
ment, traffic, challenges of living today.

I am presently in Napa, CA spending some time. I am paying attention to the areas that have been burned out by the
fire they have had in the fall of 2017. There are reasons I am
talking to home owners and getting a sense of what their future is, but there is no reason to expound upon that.   Here
is one thing that has struck me as fascinating. Most of the
folks I have talked to have talked about all the stuff they lost
and have no intentions of replacing it. The mere fact that
they don't have to "deal" with it anymore has given them a
sense of "relief."

Now the immense stress and burden of rebuilding or not
rebuilding is of course huge. But there are benefits and good
that can come out of this kind of tragedy. You just must
look for them. One of the benefits is asking yourself, "when
is enough, enough"? Is this the time to make changes in my/
our lives? Certainly, doesn't take a fire disaster to get to the
point of asking that question of yourself.

When was the last time you took a moment and looked around at all the stuff you have? If you are a hoarder, you never well. Most of us aren't hoarders, we are needers. We get way too much of what we don't need. Some folks have a lot of things. A lot.

Those that are in this state of living, normally don't use a 10th of what they have. They have shoes they don't wear, clothes that they don't wear or don't fit, tools they don't know how to use or, toys from their kids growing up 10 years ago, cars they don't drive and kitchen utensils enough for four households. This situation certainly dictates questioning a degree of sanity.

I used to have a lot of stuff. No more. I think I mentioned, I used to like to go to garage sales. Buy things I didn't need or want but buy them. Then have a garage sale often and sell if for half of what I paid for it.

Now, I only have what I use. Now grant it, I am alone, don't have someone living with me but it sure has simplified my life. Simple is where it is today in my opinion. I try to not buy to much of anything unless it can go in one end and out the other.

You want to get rid of some of the weight on your shoulders? Then get rid of the stuff that is just laying around. Garage sale first. Give it away 2nd. Give it to someone who might use it or need it 3rd. Then what is left put in on the street with a free sign. Or it goes to the dumpster if it is just junk. Most of it is.

Some people glorify in having grief and challenges in their lives. Some people wouldn't know what to do if they weren't sick all the time. Or have a head ache all the time. Or have that pain in their ass all the time. They wouldn't know what to do if they didn't have something to bitch about or a battle to fight.

They couldn't imagine getting up in the morning and looking forward to a stress free, no battles to fight, nothing to do but enjoy life kind of day. They would be tearing their hair out if their lives weren't being torn apart. All of it most of the time self-induced. Get that sticker made that goes on the bathroom mirror,

"YOU ARE LOOKING AT THE PROBLEM."

Self-induced obesity. Self-induced sickness by smoking. Eating the kinds of foods that make us sick rather than make us healthy. Drink too much. Use drugs. Hooked on prescription drugs. Deny the addiction, whatever it is. They feel glorified in the fact they are abusing themselves to the point of it being fatal. In fact, I know people who congratulate themselves and expect everyone else to because the abuse themselves and are still alive. They are proud of it. Are you one of these people?

Unfortunately, I am spending a little bit of time driving in traffic trying to help someone accomplish something business wise. It has been a long time since I fought this battle. I have done it before, many times. But today I feel and see a difference in how that battle is being fought.

Before people just seemed to go along with the flow. A sense of acceptance that traffic is a fact of life and it is part of the process.

What I see and feel now is people seem to be hell bent on getting where they are going, and they are not having fun. Everyone seems to be pissed off, angry, frustrated and ready to kill.

Seems like every driver who zips by me is on the phone. Texting, talking or doing whatever they do. Utter chaos.

Trouble is, almost every one of these drivers have no choice but to do what they are doing. Going to work or going back home from work. Or their jobs entail driving from point A to point B 50 times a day. Because if they don't, they are one week or one month away from being homeless. I would be pissed off, angry, frustrated and ready to kill too.

You talk about perfect candidates that need to be asking themselves, "when is enough, enough"?

It doesn't have to be this way. Yes, you may have to go to work. Wouldn't it be great to be able to choose to go to work? You enjoy it, because you don't have to. Or, you know you only need to do this two more years, two more months or better yet two more days.

You or you and your wife are a few of the lucky ones. You sat down 20 years ago, did the budget, kept track of where your money was going for up to a year, then did the "Life's Plan." You stuck with it and adjusted it to all the curve balls thrown at you that only life can.

The million is in the bank and investments. The house is paid off because you did a 15-year mortgage instead of a 30-year mortgage. The time is coming because you made it happen.

What is that time? When you can finally……..

"Tell the World to Kiss Your Ass."

30. YOU KNOW RIGHT FROM WRONG

This is a biggie. How many opportunities do all of us get in a day to make the decision between right and wrong? A lot. Far too often we choose the easy way out. We make the wrong decision. I am not talking about making the decision to take a right or a left from a directional stand point.

I am talking about making the decision to do right or to do wrong. A lot of people take things that don't belong to them. Is it stealing or is it kleptomania? Doesn't make a bit of difference if it is one or the other. It is wrong.

A lot of people are mean to other people. They say derogatory things, they belittle them, they try to hurt their pride and above all hurt their feelings. Why is this? I assume it is to make them feel superior and the other person inferior.

The prisons are full of both men and women that knew and know right from wrong. But they made that all defining decision to rob that store, shoot that guy, kidnap that kid, embezzle from their place of employment, drive drunk, evade taxes and bomb the mosque.

It has been said often enough so far and we are only at chapter 30 of "101 Ways." Most of us have that little guy running around in our gut that keeps us on the straight and narrow.

Most of us know right from wrong. Most of us know when we are about to make a wrong decision. The bells and whistles going off are instantaneous and they are almost always right.

After the decision has been made in a split second, then the monkey can scream, but then it is too late. A lot of wrong decisions can be reversed. An I'm sorry, give it back, pay it back, pay for it, fix it, buy a new one, whatever it takes can go a long way.

But when it comes to putting the bullet back in the gun or bringing that kid back to life you ran over driving drunk, or taking that slap back you gave your wife, or husband, or taking the words back that belittled your son or your daughter, these types of wrongs can never be rectified.

Adultery in a marriage is also a big one. Can that ever be accepted and made to go away? How? It happens. I read all the time where one spouse forgives the other and the marriage continues on a wholesome basis.

Right from wrong. It is instilled in us from an early age, perhaps as early as the womb. Our upbringing can have a lot to do with one's internal perspective of what is right and what is wrong.

Regardless of that upbringing, your gut knows. Your spirit knows. Your soul knows.

Your "Life's Plan" must be created around the right and wrong of life. Nothing will create a vehicle for failure quicker than living a life following the path of wrong versus right. The sooner it is right, the sooner you will get on top.

CHAPTER THREE: HEALTH

31. GET HEALTHY.

There are only two other words that life has taught me that could possibly be more important than "Get Healthy." Those two words are "Stay Healthy." Not one of these four words means much to you if you just turned 21. I can tell you if you are lucky in life to make it to 72, they mean everything.

Nothing matters if you aren't healthy. A good job, a good marriage, being a great father and husband or a wonderful wife and mother, a great person, loved by everybody or hated by everybody, if you don't have your health, you are miserable and doomed.

Obviously, life can throw a curve ball. You have a disease that can't be cured. Something is in your body that is hereditary. You are experiencing the luck of the draw. You are on a downward spiral with a disease and you aren't going to live long.

Or you are overweight, in fact downright fat. You eat junk food constantly, sit on your fat ass and watch TV day in and day out. It would kill you if you went for a walk farther than the refrigerator or the bathroom.

You drink and do drugs to the extreme. You are constantly in the emergency room because you have OD'd again. Even better, you just got your 6th DUI. Your wife has filed for divorce. You just got fired from your $120,000 a year job.

Healthy. Means everything. Both physically and emotionally. You can't buy it. You can't win it. It can't be given to you. You can't steal it. You can't find it. But you can earn it by doing the right things. For some people it comes naturally. It is part of their DNA. For most people it eludes them all their life. For some of us we find it thru trial and error. For some of us, life dictates we get it, or we die.

It doesn't make any difference how it comes to you. It can be naturally, work at it, find it because you want to. Or even more importantly because you must. But it is the most important aspect of your life. Make no mistake about that statement. I will say it again. Your health is the most important aspect of your life.

You want to get "Free" and be in a position to live life to the fullest.....then get healthy. You want to be a better person, father, mother, husband or wife. Then get healthy. Nothing but good comes from this simple one thing that most of us fail to realize. It leads to all kinds of success as your life goes on. Just look around you at your family, your friends, and your sphere of influence and at your place of work. What you see, unless you are one of the few is a disaster.

Go to a Walmart and just sit and watch everyone that goes in and out for an hour. It is disheartening and sickening. You can go anyplace else for that matter and you see the same thing.

When we lived in Las Vegas for years and now when I periodically fly in or out, trust me I do not go there for the Casinos, I hate the damn things, but I notice the Las Vegas Fitness Centers jam packed all hours of the day. That is great and all fine and good. Plenty more people need to make the commitment to go to these kinds of places and get fit and work towards a healthy life style.

It takes a complete whole-hearted approach and you need to cast a wide net to ensure that you capture all the things you need to do to get healthy and stay healthy. Going to the gym can be one of them but that is not necessary. There are so many things each one of us needs to do to make the transition from unhealthy to healthy.

You will never get to the point of being able to "Tell the World to Kiss Your Ass" if you don't get healthy.

32. EAT RIGHT.

This is not a book about eating right. This is a book about how to live a "happy, joyous and free" life based up on first hand experiences. A lot of years, not just a couple years gives me an edge on what works and what doesn't. You can't argue with experience. Bad or good. You can't argue with success. The adage "been there done that" still holds some water.

How many books have been written about eating right and what to eat and what not to eat? Thousands. How many make sense? Probably all of them have something in them that makes sense. But if they do, then why are there so-o-o-o-o many outright fat people in this world?

I hold to the "gut feeling" thing on eating right. I know by now what works for me and what doesn't. I know now what I eat makes all the difference in the world when it comes to what I look like, what my weight is, what makes me feel good and what makes me feel bad. I only eat what works. What makes the difference is it is the right foods? We all need to find what works and what doesn't work as individuals.

One of the best ways I have find, in conjunction with eating the right foods is I use small plates and small bowls and never have seconds. I also don't finish what is front of me just because it is there. I quit when I feel full.

Eating right is easy. It doesn't cost that much. I have cut my food bill in half by what I eat. The size of the portions now is much smaller. I have almost eliminated what I throw out that doesn't get eaten.

Eating right is another one of those "good habits" that comes easily and quickly if you make it part of your "Life's Plan." The "Life's Plan" must have a complete section on eating right. That section must be in it to make everything else in your life work in balance.

One of the surefire ways of getting in control of your life, in control of your finances and getting closer to the "big moon" is eating right.

33. DO NOT SMOKE.

If you smoke, you are flat out a complete stugoofid. Nothing in this book or any other book; nothing you hear or see; nothing anybody says is going to help you get smart and quit smoking.

No other product used by mankind kills 20 to 25% of the users of the product.

Quitting smoking for some people is impossible. I get that.

Quitting smoking for some people is easy. They just quit and get healthy.

Smoking for some people is not addiction but a learned bad habit. They don't smoke that often or that much. It is a "stress reliever" for them.

I quit smoking at 51 one year after I quit drinking. Quitting smoking did more for my health than quitting drinking. By quitting both I am sure it has saved my life.

Here is what I miss about smoking.

ABSOLUTELY NOTHING!

34. NO NOT DRINK ALCOHOL.

For a guy who drank like a fish until he was 50, I know what I am talking about. I could write a book about my experiences as an alcoholic. You nor anyone else would believe what I would have to say, but another alcoholic.

I got lucky. I quit. As I have said many times, I would take a bullet before I ever drank again.

If you are an alcoholic and you know it, as well as ever one else, you need to do something about it. Just quit. Get some help. Now.

Then you will have a chance to get your "Life's Plan" in order and start to live a happy, joyous and "free" life. Until then, it is nothing but chaos and trouble. Imprisonment, death or insanity is normally the outcome. That is just a fact.

If you are a social drinker my hat is off to you. When is too much alcohol too much? To anyone who must ask that question, you probably already know the answer to that question.

Chances are if you have been asked that question or you are asking yourself that question, you need to evaluate where your relationship stands with alcohol.

Alcohol can end up being one of the biggest contributors to never getting "Free" and having nothing but chaos in your life as a direct result of too much alcohol intake.

I cannot come up with one productive thing that out all my years of alcohol abuse, spending time in night clubs and bars and having blow out parties gave me. Not one single thing. I do know I wasted most of the good years of my life under the influence of alcohol and all the ramifications that came from it.

You want to hear something from a guy who once again has been there and done that. Don't drink at all. You won't miss it once it becomes part of your past life.

There is no redeeming value from drinking alcohol. None.

35. DO NOT CHEW.

Sounds like I am preaching doesn't it? Giving advice perhaps? Not true. I am just letting the reader know a few things I have learned over the last 55 years or so. I have never preached or given advice. I try to do by example.

Admittedly the first 35 years of my life I didn't do too well by example. The last 20 plus years I hope I have impacted somebody's life positively. Lucky me to have got it, falling thru the cracks, as I like to say and landing on my feet.

I chewed once. Puked all over Pete Dengenus's car who was the football coach at Bend High School in Bend, Oregon. I had returned from spending some time in Europe after getting out of Vietnam. I was taking another stab at college going to Central Oregon Community College and happen to be living with Pete. What a great guy. Both he and Gary Olson, the other football coach both chewed tobaccos. Naturally I had to try it. It was just that once and never again.

But what really cured me was when I got into the VA Health System. I kept seeing these guys with no lips, no throats, half their face missing, and I thought it was all combat related.

It wasn't. They chewed tobacco.

Need I say more?

Chewing tobacco is like smoking. You must be a stugoofid to

keep chewing. Are you?

One of the biggest mysteries I see is the nurse or the doctor out behind the hospital smoking. They see the death and sicknesses caused by smoking day in and day out, but they go out back and SMOKE.

Just my opinion, don't get judgmental.

36. GO FOR A WALK DAILY.

I can't think of anything that has done more for both my physical health and my emotional health than going for a walk. Except for quitting drinking and smoking.

I try to go at least four or more miles daily. There are days I just can't get to it and it never ends up being as good of day as the days I go for a walk.

It is the number one personal joy of my life. I am confident the walking has been one of the primary factors where my health is at the age of 72. I can tell you my health is in a good place.

I tried running and it just didn't work for me. I used to get up at 4:30AM every morning and run with Lt. General Rosson in Vietnam when I was his driver and enlisted aide. But I was 19/20 years old. That is when I probably got it into my system that getting up early and getting exercise was a good thing.

I prefer to walk out in nature, in the mountains, along the rivers, into the desert and among the animals, the birds and the trees. I can't imagine walking in town, where you have all the noise of the traffic and the chaos.

It has helped me stay fit and trim. It has helped keep me keep fit and trim. It has helped give me a complete peace of mind. It has given me an edge.

I know my life is in balance, grounded and centered when I go for a walk and I feel like I am walking on air. That is how good I feel these days. It propels me forward in my life. It has helped put me in a good frame of mind. That is what walking does for me.

It is close to the number one thing in my life that gives me the happy, joyous and free feeling. It puts me in a command influence frame of mind to "Tell the World to Kiss My Ass."

37. EXERCISE DAILY.

Exercising daily is probably one of the most difficult things to do and make it a habit day in and day out. I prefer the early mornings because I am an early morning person.

I don't exercise every day and I miss it when I don't. At 72 years old it really makes a difference if the exercising daily happens and not too many days are missed. The biggest thing I regret about exercising is I didn't start it sooner in my life. Being a drinker and a smoker up till the age of 50 wasn't conducive to be an exerciser.

With working, kids, spouses, the commute to work, weekend plans, it is just a difficult thing as busy as everyone is these days. Then when you throw in the Facebook, Snapchat, Texting, Emails, Selfies, Twitter, Likenden and life itself, no wonder there are very few people make exercising part of the must be done daily routine. Throw in TV and gaming that a lot of people do, exercise just isn't going to happen.

Spend an hour or two sitting out front of a Wal Mart. If that doesn't convince you to start exercising nothing well.

I say to anyone who will just think about it, exercising is part of getting and staying healthy. Without good health everything else goes out the window.

Getting totally "Free" means you must get healthy. Which means you must exercise, consistently. It can be just a routine of stretching, walking, yoga, perhaps some light running. Bicycle riding on two wheels or stationary. Lifting some weights. It doesn't make any difference what it is, but it must be something.

Using your lunch hour is also another good way to get some walking around the building or up and down the stairwells in. The older you get the more important it is. Unfortunately, a lot of folks get over weight. They don't do anything about it. They get over the hill and they can't come back to the top and down the other side. That's it for them. They are done. It is only a matter of time.

There is no way in hell you will ever get "Free" enough "To Tell the World to Kiss Your Ass" if you don't make exercising part of your "Life's Plan" on the road to total freedom.

38. TAKE SOME TIME FOR YOURSELF.

Until I got sober, I didn't realize how important I was to myself. Nothing, nobody, no amount of money can replace understanding who you are. What makes you tick? What makes you happy? What makes you angry? Most important of all, how should you be conducting your life, for you?

This can only happen with some life's experiences. Evaluating those life experiences and reaping full benefit from them. A lot of what we do early on in life has consequences. Some of these consequences can teach us something. Or we just keep on making decisions that is the result of another consequence.

The sooner we learn that there are decisions we can make in life that reward us, the sooner control becomes a part of our life. Good health, good friendships, a good marriage, healthy relationships, respect of others, communication with our kids, a good income, the list can and does go on and on. They are not the same for all of us. But it is a known fact, we are all pretty much the same when you get right down to it. The fact is we have choices. We can make decisions that will either reward us or punish us.

Most always there is a chance to make the right decision. It might be only a fraction of a second. But it normally is always there. Unfortunately, more often than not, the wrong decision is made.

Reflecting on how our life is going is essential. Spending that all important time in the bathroom becomes very productive. Asking ourselves what can I do to make things better? More productive? More rewarding? More profitable? Make me happier? Get healthier? Get along with people better? Get a raise from work, or a kind word for my spouse.

If you spend all day with your face in your phone, or your face in the computer on Facebook, or sitting on your butt every night watching TV, chances are it has been quite a while since you spent any time with the most important person in your life. You.

I don't know about you, but I would rather have the opportunity to bend over every night and "Tell the World to Kiss My Ass", than know before I went to bed I just spent 4 hours sitting on it.

39. TREAT YOUR MIND AND BODY IF IT WERE THE ONLY ONE YOU WILL EVER HAVE, IT IS!

Every day I am constantly appreciative of how well I feel and how active I am and the amount of physical activities I can do and do well. My mind and my body have no clue they have reached 72 years of age. I read an article the other day about "ageless seniors." The number one thing that is keeping seniors that don't appear to be aging, is they keep their mind and their bodies active.

When we are young, unfortunately the things that really count, particularly later in life, we just don't pay enough or any attention to. The number one thing above all else is our health. Some of us just naturally get lucky and no matter what we do to our bodies, we live to a ripe old age. However, it is very few compared to the many that die young because they didn't pay enough attention to their health.

We all know there are those of us that have the luck of the draw against us and no matter what we do we get that cancer, or have that heart attack, or get hit by that car or that sack of shit falls from the sky and it is all over.

But for the most of us who do make it, let's say to 65, and we haven't been hit up beside the head, our health becomes the number one issue in our lives we care about, or we should if we care to live at all.

I know a lot of my friends all died at a young age, except for one that died at 86. Several of them died because of treating their mind and their body like it belonged to their worst enemy.

When I look around at the population today, I swear, most people have a death wish. The way they drink alcohol to excess, the kinds of foods they are eating, the number of drugs both prescription and street drugs taken is astounding. Their life style, their lack of activities both mental and physical only determines one outcome, death and death sooner than later.

Being healthy not only involves your physical health, your mental health is just as important. Keeping active learning new things, reading, having a variety of hobbies that keep you seeking new information is just as important as to what you place in front of you to eat and put into your body.

Once again, and I will say it 100 times before I am thru.

Watching TV is not a hobby.

Watching TV is not healthy nor is it a part of your daily physical exercising routine.

Watching TV isn't going to stimulate your mind or your body.

Watching TV will be the biggest contributor to your death wish.

I am having so much fun and enjoying this period of my life way beyond what I ever imagined. To anyone who is a thinker and will listen, it is so far, the best time in my life. I try to have as little stress as possible. I work daily to anticipate the situations that do stress me out and avoid them those situations with careful planning.

It has become a habit to live well. Live a healthy lifestyle. Exercise daily. Eat the foods that I know are good for me. Schedule my life around doing the things that gives me almost daily the "joyous, happy and free" I strive for and have been lucky enough to find.

I don't care who you are. Unless you are over the hill, way over and no matter what you do you can't get up over the top to the other side. The sooner you start to make your health your #1 priority, the sooner you can do these other things that will get you, "FREE."

You can give thanks to all, far and wide. You can go outside in the back yard. Stand on the porch. Go out in the middle of the field.

Doesn't make any difference where it ends up being. There is no greater joy in the world than "Telling it to Kiss Your Ass."

CHAPTER FOUR: WORK

40. PICK A CAREER EARLY ON IN LIFE THAT HOPEFULLY IS THE RIGHT ONE.

The earlier in life you can sit down and start on your "Life's Plan" the better off you are going to be. What you want to do to earn an income, support a family, plan for your future is paramount. It doesn't have to be cast in stone if you are only 18. Even if you are in your early 20's it isn't going to end up the way you envision it. But without a doubt, the earlier you start thinking about the path you want to take to get to a point of being "Free" the better off you are going to be.

I know a few younger people that have money. Their family had money and they got some of it, or all of it at an early age. They are just as lost without something to do, a plan if you well as the person who doesn't have that kind of money or a plan. In fact, at times they are miserable. They don't have to work, but they want to do something that puts meaning in their life. Money will never replace the feeling of "self worth."

Are you going to be a worker? A person who gets a paycheck and structures their life around that consistent income. Or are you going to be in financial sector of the economy? An accountant perhaps? In the medical profession? How about in the energy sector of the economy?

Maybe it is starting your own business. That is huge these days. Drive around and make yourself aware of all the small business-es that are supporting families. It is mind boggling.

It is not easy these days trying to decide what you want to do or what your career is going to be. Things change so fast and things come and go that what you think might be isn't going to be 10 years down the road. So, it could be a moving target. College or no college? College and working at the same time are a challenge but it is done and accomplished all the time.

Is it a doctor or a small engine repair person? Computers or rockets? Jets or drones? The Army or the Air Force? The submarines or the marines? How about cancer research? The choices are endless. The reasons for making those choices are even more endless and complex. It does matter what it is. Taking the time to research, go look and see, feel it and smell is what will make that choice more likely to succeed than fail.

I have always been a good one for a "New View." What I thought was going to work sometimes didn't. I never hesitated to make that move. Take that new job. Start that new business. Be challenged and go for the outcome no matter what it might end up being. I had no fear. I was often accused of being un-stable. I was asked many times, "what is it you are looking for"?

I had no idea what I was looking for. My problem was I didn't have a "Life's Plan." I had absolutely no clue or plan when it came to a career, a family or financial stability. Absolutely nothing was thought out.

I started my life after Vietnam with no idea what so ever. None.
Never even crossed my mind to plan and make it a life's endeav-
or to achieve anything other than what I could see. What I am
expounding upon here in this book is not something I haven't
experienced. There isn't much that hasn't crossed my path that
gives me some idea of what I am talking about.

This doesn't have to be hard. I am not saying it is easy. But having a
plan for anything is much easier that walking out the door and not
knowing if you are going to go east, west, north or south.

The hardest part of walking across the United States is taking
that 1st step. People do walk across the United States. But they
would never get to the other side of the country if they hadn't
have taken that 1st step. The 1st real step in your life ought to
be your "Life's Plan."

You got to get serious. No matter where you are in life. If you
haven't retired yet, there is a way to make the rest of your life
easier. It obviously is going to require making some changes
and perhaps even sacrificing for awhile.

But remember, nothing last forever. Nothing.

41. START A SMALL BUSINESS.

By suggesting you start a business, I am referring to starting a business that you work full time in, not work and have a small business at home. Not that the small business at home you start isn't really a business, but you are at the same time also working.

You must know what the new business is going to be. If you are inclined towards being inside and are a computer nerd, chances are you are it isn't going to be a good idea to start a landscaping business. These days done right, you won't ever see a "poor" landscaping business owner. Or a poor computer business owner for that matter. I called a guy the other day to help me on something and he was at $150 an hour and couldn't get to me for a month.

Just like your life, no business should ever be started without a very detailed business plan. In fact, doing a business plan for you new business should be easy for you because now you have the experience of just completing your "Life's Plan." Business plans and life's plans are a moving target and are somewhat alike. They change like the four seasons. Where the problem comes in and the failures start to mount up, is when you don't take the time to adapt and change the plan to the present-day circumstances. It is a life killer and it is a business killer to not keep up on what it takes to adapt.

Don't ever contemplate starting a business on borrowed money. The success of that business is almost guaranteed to fail. You can't start out in debt. It doesn't mean once you get up and the business is thriving and surviving on the cash flow that there can't be credit used to expand, buy or lease new equipment, start a 2nd location, whatever makes sense. But it can't be done on a whim. The business plan must be updated to reflect all the positives and negatives of making those kinds of decisions.

Are you going to have employees? Having employees is a big deal. Many a new business has failed because it didn't consider the expense of having employees. Having employees is not cheap. Go spend some time with a business owner that must make payroll every Friday. For some businesses it is easy. The cash flow is consistent and can be counted on. Other businesses, such as construction is a whole different story. Their cash flow is not consistent, nor can it ever be counted on. If you are considering starting a construction related business, I would go spend at least a month with the owner of one, work for one and get a feel for just what a challenge it is. Being a construction worker and owning a construction company are entirely two different things.

Is it a franchise? There are lots of them to choose from. The business plan is already done, financing can be an option, the idea is there, the equipment, the advertising, the signage, not much to have to do but write the check out.

If you are married is the new business going to be a husband and wife thing? Or does one spouse continue to work to guarantee income coming into the household? Unless you got lots of money in the savings account, just inherited money or won the lottery, for both of you to quit working is dangerous.

This whole scenario goes back to what I said before. 8 out of 10 workers in this country live paycheck to paycheck. If you are living paycheck to paycheck, not much wiggle room in that situation to start a new business.

No one ever said it was going to be easy. It is going to take a lot of work. Go spend more time in the bathroom with the door closed looking in the mirror if you aren't quite convinced yet.

42. ALWAYS SHOW UP TO WORK EARLY. BE THE LAST ONE TO LEAVE.

You can stand out and be the guy or gal that is noticed. Or you can just be one of the workers. Showing up early and being the last one to leave is a good way to let your boss, your company, your co-workers or your manager know you appreciate your job. Being late, leaving early is a sure-fire way of letting them know you don't appreciate your job and you could care less.

Doing what no one else well do is another good way to stand out. Maybe you aren't the kind of person who wants to stand out and I am not saying you should be. But I know from owning a lot of businesses with a lot of employees over the years it wasn't hard to determine who I could count on and who I couldn't. I also have had a lot of experiences as an employee. I always strived to be there early and never got in a hurry to leave. It always made a difference in the way I was treated and the income I received.

It is a matter of respect. It also is a showing of how much you respect yourself. That is where it all begins. How much you respect yourself. If you are late for work, it shows a lack of respect for yourself first. This whole process of getting "Free" has to do with respect. Respect for yourself. Respect for your family. Respect for your relationships. Respect and appreciation for the money you earn and keep. Respect for the process of getting "Free."

You will never get "Free" if you disrespect the process by being late for work, late for appointments and for sure disrespecting what money can do for you. You can go thru life with nothing or you can get to a point, very fast in your life where the accumulation of having financial security gives you a huge edge. It gives you an edge in what you decide to do with it. Where you go and what you do. Having financial security gives you a huge advantage. It means you can to change careers; change jobs, move to another part of the country to better your life and your families. Without this advantage you are stuck. A lot of people are stuck forever. The biggest reason is because they just won't make a commitment. Then once they make the commitments, they won't live up to them.

They need to spend more time in the bathroom looking in the mirror. I used to give out a little sticker for folks to put on the right-hand bottom of their mirror in the bathroom. It was the first thing they saw every morning.

It said: "You are looking at the problem."

43. WORKING OR OWNING A BUSINESS CAN BE THE KEY TO MAKING YOU FREE. PLAN...PLAN...PLAN.

It is imperative that you find out where all your money is going. You must commit to completing the "Life's Plan." You must do a budget. You must stick to that budget. You have got to adapt to life's curve balls. If you aren't true to yourself and live up to the commitments necessary to make all this work, then you will remain or become one of the 8 out of 10 workers in this country that live pay check to pay check. Not much of an up-lifting situation.

With doing the "Life's Plan", the budget and making the commitments then you are ready to make the decisions necessary to move forward. Am I in the right job? Do I need to go back to school and get a degree in? Should we move to another part of the country where we can live for less and make more money? Should we, should we, should we? Without a "Life's Plan" asking those questions is never going to lead to finding the answers.

Do I/we finally start that business we have always wanted to? Does it make sense or is a just a pipe dream? Planning, talking to those with experience, researching, working at it will get those answers you are seeking. You can't beat experience. There is nothing you are going to do that somebody else hasn't done many times over. Don't reinvent the wheel as they say.

Owning a small business or a big business for that matter is not for everyone. I was a great one for spotting opportunities. I was a lousy business man. I just lost interest in the day to day running of the business. My excitement came from the idea of the business. Getting it started and making it happen. The on-going success of the business was something I just wasn't good at. I was always looking for the next thing to get me excited.

Planning is where it is all at. That is where it starts. It is much easier today to do this planning than it was years ago without having the internet and all the information/experience available. There is just no reason at all that planning isn't part of your life in every aspect of it when it comes to executing the "Life's Plan" and laying out the roadmap to getting "Free."

Where this all becomes fun is when you start to see the results of the planning. Your health improves. You have more free time to do what you should be doing. Your relationships improve with everyone. Your savings account and investment portfolio are growing.

There is nothing bad that comes out of any of this. It is all positive, good and rewarding.

CHAPTER FIVE:
FAMILY AND RELATIONSHIPS

44.THINK VERY HARD BEFORE BECOMING A WIFE/HUSBAND OR A MOTHER/FATHER.

The family and relationships chapter are the reason that it has taken me 15 years to complete this endeavor. I have never been good at either. At times I wonder if I even have a clue what it takes to have a good relationship with my four children. I still don't have a clue on what it takes to be a good husband. It is by far the number one thing in my life I struggle with.

You would think a 72-year-old guy would just let it pass and move on. But it consumes a lot of my time and what I think about. It is deeply depressing at times. We all wish we could do things differently in some aspects of our life when we get older. This for me is one of those things I would really like to get another shot at.

I was very deficient in both from day one. There is no doubt in my mind that the number one reason for that is I never had any kind of plan when I got back one from Europe after traveling around for 6/7 months, after spending the 26 months in Vietnam. It gets to the heart of this book and why I think it is so important to have a "Life's Plan" before embarking on getting married, having a family and cultivating personal as well as business relationships.

My entire life in the early 20's was consumed by partying, drinking, having fun…just one big party. It went on for years and years and years. In fact, I hate to admit it, but it didn't end until after my 50th birthday party. Yes, there were times when I started businesses. I was an employer, as well as an employee. But nothing got in the way of the boozing and craziness. Nothing.

When I look back on how things have gone about the family and relationships part of my life, I just wish I would have had some direction from somebody. I didn't. It just happened daily. No thought was really put into any kind of planning for down the road. I never had a problem making money. I certainly didn't have a problem spending it. If I could see the dollars at the end of the next day I knew I had it made. I always was working or making sure there was enough money to support myself. Once I got married it was no different. My first wife and I didn't ever sit down and say, ok, here is the plan. Just didn't happen. I never even had a notion of doing it. What a mistake.

Nor did it happen with my second wife Debbie. No discussions of long-term plans. NO "LIFE'S PLAN." I regret it immensely because I feel it is why we are no longer together. I am not happy about that at all. Sure…there are other factors in that relationship…but.

That mistake has made the difference between chaos and upheaval versus serenity and peace in both my personal life and my life as a father and a two-time husband. Now I am not saying that life would have been all peaches and cream to be sure. But I can tell you all this. It would have been a whole lot easier if I would have been following a well laid out "Life's Plan." I know that for a fact. Because I would have been an excellent planner and executer of that plan you will ever find.

The "Life's Plan" must be the single most important thing you can do as you start to live your life as a responsible adult. The whim thing normally doesn't work out to well. Responsible is the key word here. Anything less than responsible is not going to be a whole lot of fun. It is common sense and the right thing to do. It is probably one of the simplest things you will ever do but solves some of the biggest problems in life that are in all our lives.

The biggest part of all of this is that time….time just goes by so fast. Before you know it, decades have gone by and not a whole lot of substance to show for it. A lot of us think we have a lot to show for it. There are the cars, the house, the crap lying around, the toys, the boats, the s-t-u-f-f. You are still married with 3 children that you see and spend some time with. But just think how different it could have been if some of us would have started out with a plan.

What I am also referring to is the security of a sound relationship with your spouse.   Having an enduring and lasting relationship with your children and the grandchildren is something I have missed. Having friends who you can do things with and you enjoy spending time with is also something I don't have.   Most importantly there is the financial security. These things in my opinion just don't happen. You must work at them and plan for them to happen.

45. RESPECT EACH OTHER.

As I attempt to go thru the next several chapters of this book, it is going to be one of the most difficult things I have ever done. I have read a lot of books, searched the internet and talked to a variety of people on these two subjects. The conclusion I have come to is this:

I certainly missed a lot of joy in my life by not having a clue when it came to children and marriage.

I am not going to try impress upon on that I am a marriage counselor now. The only thing I know is I don't know much. But I am certain of this. To achieve any amount of "Freedom" or your "Life's Plan", if you are married or thinking about getting married, then a successful marriage is a huge part of accomplishing the "Plan."

You will never get to a point of "Telling the World to Kiss Your Ass" if you don't succeed at the marriage thing. Assuming you stay married. Or get married again and again and again.

No relationship or marriage can withstand disrespect. We all know what respect is. It is ingrained in us right from the beginning. What is sad a lot of folks grow up in an environment where there was no respect. We all learn from our parents. We only know what we know. I grew up in a house that had respect. I am pretty sure I did. But did I respect both of my spouses? As I look back on all those years, I am not so certain my actions showed a lot of respect.

I would give a lot right now for having the opportunity have some planning and vision at about 23 years old. But now I know, as I approach all this living alone at my age, it is easier to face the music alone; than it is having someone else you must accommodate.

However, I would rather have the opportunity to accommodate, than be alone, if that makes sense. But all of this isn't about me. It is about you and how best you can live your life.

Sharing your life with your spouse and get to a point you can be "Free." That just isn't going to happen. It is going to take a lot of planning, dedication and work on both of those in a marriage.

If you will put as much effort into working at your budget and you're "Life's Plan" as you do in other endeavors in your life, you will succeed. Doesn't mean those other things have to be neglected or given up. But it is a combined task. Sit down together and just do it. It is simple. It doesn't take that much time or effort. The results will be astounding immediately.

You have got to get rid of the bad habits.

Disrespecting your spouse or your significant other is a bad habit.

46. HAVE A DEEP EXPRESSION OF APPRECIATION

It is one thing to appreciate someone and only you know it. You never take the time to express that appreciation in words and deeds. You just assume since you are present that is showing the appreciation. We all crave and need the expression of appreciation. It is normally the little things that make the difference in a marriage. It is also the little things in a marriage that seem insignificant and can jeopardize or even ruin the relationship.

It can be something as simple as holding her or his hand. It can be something as simple as a smile…or that look. A thank you can go a very long way. Please, can also can go miles in showing appreciation. Respecting your mate is at the top in the appreciation category.

When I look back on the beginning of both of my marriages, the most significant way I could have shown respect and appreciation was to immediately sit down and do the budget and the start the "Life's Plan." Nothing would have shown either one of them how much I appreciated and respected them more than letting her know I had both of our best interests in mind.

We were going to have a plan that insured we were going to succeed. The plan doesn't have to be cast in concrete. That is impossible. It will be a work in progress. Just like the marriage is a work in progress. Things change. Things happen. Jobs are gotten and lost. Careers are started and end and another one begins. There is a move that takes place across the country. Parents die and that can change a lot of things. People get sick. But there is one thing that will always stand fast. If you have a "Life's Plan"… and you are working that plan diligently together, your marriage has a much better chance of staying on the course.

47. THE SUCCESS OF THE "LIFE'S PLAN" AS WELL AS THE MARRIAGE/RELATIONSHIP IS ATTRIBUTABLE TO BOTH PARTNERS.

If you aren't sailing the ship alone and most of us don't start out alone, then everything pretty much is a dual challenge. Meaning, it takes both of you to make this thing work. That is why it is so important after you get married and a routine settles in, you have got to sit down and start working the budget and an outline for the "Life's Plan."

There is something to be said about a routine if it is a good one. As I look back on my various routines on how I lived my life, there was up until I got sober after I turned 50, some routines that left a lot to be desired. In other words, the routines I had were bad ones and it took a lot of work and resolve to break them. It wasn't easy. But I did. As life got easier it became very apparent there certainly was an easier way to make things work, to accomplish the daily goals, I set as well as the medium and long-term goals.

Bad habits are always easier to live with than good habits. I believe from experience that bad habits are much easier to do than good habits.

But it is the good habits that bring success and rewards so easily. It has always baffled me why then did I seem to always surround myself with bad habits.

One person in the marriage/relationship can't have good habits and the other person have bad habits. It just won't work.

Never has and never well. Both must strive and make commitments to support each other. You must share in the common goal of participating and working within the confines of good habits. Both must participate in the budget, in the "Life's Plan" and in the successes when the goals are achieved.

I am not quite sure what the statistics say, but I think well over 50% of marriages these days end up in divorce. Probably considerably more. The reasons for that is a mile long. But on that list, I am sure some place there is the fact that "this couple" didn't share their ideas, their goals and didn't contribute equally to the relationship and didn't even have a plan, let alone an idea of a plan.

There is one good thing about living within your means as a married couple. Having a "Life's Plan" and succeeding in executing that "Life's Plan" the good thing is this:

If, for whatever reason the marriage ends up in divorce there will be some assets there for both of you to move on with. Because that is what it is. Moving on with your life. One would hope that the lessons learned will be noted and the mistakes made won't be repeated.

The chances of your marriage surviving are far greater by putting in some quality time together and communicating.

Take turns in the bathroom looking in the mirror. Make sure you pay attention to that little note over on the bottom of the right-hand side.

48. THERE SHOULD BE A SPIRITUAL CONNEC-TION.

I have never been one for the church thing or big on religion. I have tried at times. As I look back on things, time has afforded me to wonder why that was. It was a mistake from my perspective at this point in my life. If I had the opportunity to do it over, I would have taken another route.

A marriage/relationship that has a spiritual connection, a religious based faith is by far stronger than if it doesn't exist. I consider it to be one of my biggest faults. I believe it must be part of the "Life's Plan." It is one of the aspects in life that bonds two people together. Gives them something to do together and gives them a completely different perspective in life when it is part of the marriage/relationship. You must make up your own mind on this one. But experience is the best teacher in almost all aspects of life. It is just too bad individuals, couples and for sure a country very seldom learns from their mistakes.

I can't speak from experience on this because neither one of my two marriages were faith based. I am convinced that it strengthens a marriage/relationship. I can tell you this though. My spiritual connection it is the biggest part of my life as a sober man and makes a marriage/relationship much stronger.

It makes it more fun to share the accomplishments and to see the results of executing the plan. It doesn't take long. Once it begins it becomes that a snowball going downhill. It is like a freight train with no breaks going down the mountain.

The successes just keep getting bigger and bigger and bigger and happening faster and faster and faster and before long, you both are out in the back yard, bending over and "Telling the World to Kiss Your Ass."

49. BOTH AGREE THE RELATIONSHIP TAKES CONSTANT WORK AND ATTENTION.

If it is worth doing, then it is going to take a lot of work and attention. All along I have been saying that to accomplish your goals and reach the end of the rainbow you have got to put the time in and make the commitment. Making the commitment is just the beginning. Living up to that commitment is where the difference comes in. No different in a marriage or relationship. It just isn't easy folks, particularly these days. Finances, hurricanes, floods, fires and terrorists, along with just the constant pressures of making enough money to make ends meet is a constant challenge.

It doesn't have to be hard. Yes, there are going to be the jobs lost, vehicles break down, flat tires, dead batteries, health issues, death, sickness, hurricanes, floods, fires and challenges. But that is life.

Remember the "Life's Plan" is all encompassing and it is there to protect you and your family. Just living within your means and working with your budget daily is just part of getting "Free." Getting "Free" is all encompassing. You have choices once you get "Free."

Communication between the two of you is more than essential. It is critical to the success of the marriage/relationship along with the success of living within the budget and accomplishing the goals set for in the "Life's Plan." It takes constant work and daily attention. If the two of you are still sitting around and watching TV and talking to the news commentator or laughing at Ellen, then you are going to continually have problems. You need to be working on how things are going and strategizing on the next stage of the plan. Are you living within the confines of the budget? Both of you need to answer that question and do what is necessary to make sure the answer is yes.

Would you rather be one of the few or just one of the many?

50. BE WHO YOU ARE.

You can't change who you are. You can improve on who you are or even worse, you can become somebody you aren't. One the most difficult things I have observed over the years in my marriage as well as other marriages both individuals in the marriage/relationship just won't accept who they are. They try to be what others see them as. Or one or the other tries to change the other one into who they would like them to be.

Far too often the person we married doesn't turn out to be the person we thought they were. That is why, and make no mistake about this....sitting down before you get married and work on a future budget and on the "Life's Plan" can save a whole lot of grieve down the road. Now...you can just get married, ignore it, plod along for the 1st 5 or 10 years and accomplish nothing.

Or you can put the time and planning in beforehand and you both suddenly realizes that you have entirely two different ideas on how money should be spent and saved. A 1,200 sq ft house for one might be a 2,600 sq ft house for the other. For one a new car is a must, while for the other a 10-year-old car is fine. Going out to eat at least six times a week is how one is used to eating, while the other one doesn't care if he or she ever goes out to dinner. A big one is one sleeps in till 10 in the morning, the other is out of bed and doing something by 5 AM.

Compromising is a great way to start out a marriage. But normally compromising is a quick fix. Compromises don't tend to last. That is because we all are creatures of habit. Good or bad, that is what we are used to. It takes a lot of effort and time to break the process of living in a bad habit world.

When you take in to consideration all the challenges of just getting a job these days, I just don't see how anybody can start out without doing some due diligence and put forth the effort to make sure you are compatible. It takes more effort and work at making something work well, than it does to just let life go by without putting forth any effort. You just end up like the other 8 out of 10 working Americans that live pay check to pay check.

Start out right. Start out the 1st week of your marriage living within your budget and at the end of the 1st year you will be on track to retire when you want to. It is not out of the question to retire in your 40's or 50's at all. Just take a plan and making sure you stick to the plan. It is that easy.

True and lasting love only exists by loving yourself first, knowing who you are. You can only get from another person what you're willing to give yourself.

Why would you not want to start out right from the beginning of the marriage instead of doing nothing making it so difficult everyone suffers continually?

51. ENJOY BEING WITH YOURSELF.

A lot of people have trouble being alone. That is why you see the mall so crowded. I have been in New Orleans when it wasn't even Mardi Gras and they were shoulder to shoulder in the French Quarter. It is also why you see them living in places like LA. No way could they drive down the freeway by themselves. They couldn't handle it. Those kind of people need the traffic and the chaos to make them feel wanted. Or a part of something.

Then when it comes time for their husband or wife to go do something with their friends or the kids, they fall to pieces because they are alone. They can't function. They don't accomplish anything. It is depression time.

One of the biggest obstacles to getting "Free" and getting to the point of "Telling the World to Kiss Your Ass", is not being able to enjoy being with yourself. You must get over it. It is just another one of those learned processes. Getting rid of another bad habit and starting to live another good habit. Find those things to do that one does by themselves. Walking, running, bike riding, painting, do some yard work, paint the house, wash the windows, volunteer at the church, help at the Girls and Boys club. Go out in the wilderness for a weekend. Then go for a week.

You must let your wife, husband or partner breathe. That in turn lets you breathe. Then when it comes time to spend time together it is quality time. No better-quality time than reviewing the budget and see where you stand on accomplishing the goals in you're "Life's Plan." That obviously is good quality time you spend together. Assuming you can do it without arguing and any animosity. What a great thing it is for both of you to realize you are accomplishing your goals and finding that out together.

Even though I believe we are creatures of habit and we rarely change who we are as time goes on, we need to analyze who we have become. Are you the person you want others to see?

Do you respect yourself and the way you act and treat others? If you don't, then certainly you can't expect others to respect you. Then that downward spiral starts and sometimes it just doesn't stop.

Be yourself. Like whom you are. If you look in the mirror and you don't see that person looking back at you…you want to be…then you have some work to do.

52. ARE WE HAVING FUN YET?

We all make deals with ourselves. There are many times
when the bullets were flying in Vietnam I told the Lord if
he would just get me out of this one, things would change.
They never did. Most of us never live up to the deals we
make with ourselves. It is easy to do, because nobody else
knows. But it is the deals we make with ourselves that we
don't live up to that cause the most problems. It is a very bad
habit of the worst kind.

Until you start living up to the commitments you make with
yourself, you will never live up to the deals you make with
others. Never. Not your wife, your husband, your mother, your father, your business partner, your customer, your
friend, your brother or sister, no one. Your life will continue
to be nothing but one big cluster event.

To make it even more challenging, if you are married, now
there are two of you. Making deals with yourself and each
other. If you have the bad habit of saying you are going to
do this and do that, and you never do, imagine what it is
going to be like now when you start telling your wife or husband you are going to do this and do that and never do?

The first important commitment I ever lived up to, that
I made with myself was when I got sober. I told myself I
was never going to do anything I didn't want to that would
jeopardize my sobriety and put me at risk. I have never let

myself down on that one. As time has gone on, I have found it easier and easier to commit to things that are positive, healthy and rewarding and do them.

Once you get over the first one and hopefully that deal you make with yourself is life changing, then rest comes much easier. If drugs, alcohol, infidelity, lying, cheating, stealing, dishonesty, insanity and just plan old laziness is involved, you have some reckoning to do in the bathroom. Nothing is going to happen from a positive stand point until you get clean and positive in every way.

Once you have solved one or more and all the issues the fun can begin.

Imagine having the first six months of your "Life's Plan" behind you? You did it together. Husband and Wife. You have together kept track of where all your money is being spent. You worked together to create the first beginnings of a budget that allows you to start saving money and live within your means. Things seem to be working much smoother around the house. The stress on pay day isn't there like it used to be. You aren't fighting over money any more. You both are doing what you say you are going to.

You trust each other.

53. LOVING EACH OTHER IS NOT GOING TO BE ENOUGH.

I don't think it has ever has been. There is more to a marriage/relationship than just loving each other. No amount of love is going to overcome addictions, infidelity, lack of respect, financial hardships, meanness, dishonestly, too much TV and probably one of the big ones is complacency.

Initially of course sex and intimacy are the biggies. That never lasts long. Then reality sets in. She finds out he farts in bed in his sleep. He finds out she snores like a logger. She gains 80 pounds. He starts smoking and drinking.

Then complacency sets in and seven years have gone by and the itch starts. The trouble in paradise has begun. No communication or sitting down and trying to put the finger on the pulse of the marriage/relationship.

But let's step back five or six years here for a moment. Would there be a difference at the seven years if there had been the communication in the beginning? The "Life's Plan" was perfected and was being followed and changed as the years have gone by. Would that have made a difference? I think so. No, I know so.

It certainly isn't going to overcome the farting and snoring but it sure would go a long way in giving the marriage/relationship a pulse. You can solve the idiosyncrasies by diet, exercise and the like. What you can't do is get the time back. It is impossible.

A couple that lets this go on for a long time can't get back up and over. It is too late. Thirty years have gone by. If they are lucky enough they are still married, or unlucky whatever the case may be. They are doomed to despair and destitution.

One Sunday morning he just can't take anymore of the grief and he beats her to death with the cast iron skillet. Or she walks in the kitchen while he wants to know where breakfast is, and she shoots him dead. Her comment to the officer, as he was putting her in the back of the police car was, "I just couldn't take it anymore." Could all of this have been prevented by a "Life's Plan"? I would rather have one to have been living by…than one not at all.

Loving each other is just not going to be enough.

It never has been and never will be.

Sit down, get started on the budget and the "Life's Plan."

Prove how much you love each other.

54. HAVING CHILDREN IS A HUGE RESPONSIBILITY.

Do I think having children should be planned? Yes. Did my 1st wife and I? No. We just had them, and we had 5. The 1st son, Brad drowned at 16 months old in an irrigation ditch in Bend Oregon. Cameron was born not long after the drowning. Angie was born in Anchorage, Alaska. The last two, Chrissi and Lavonne were born after I had a vasectomy when we were living in Fossil, Oregon. When I went back and had the 2nd vasectomy that one worked. My good friend, Doctor Luelling in Madras, Oregon had missed the left side. I went to the University of Oregon with Doug before I joined the Army in 1966.

When I look back on all of that, never do I remember Cheryl and I sitting down and discussing the "future" when it came to children. Nor do I remember us ever sitting down and discussing anything that had to do the well being of all of us. Shame on me.

Did my second wife Debbie and I sit down and talk about this? Yes. I even went so far as to have a reversal on the vasectomies. We tried for years to have a baby. Wasn't meant to be. Did we go much further than that on the aspect of a "Life's Plan." No. Shame on me again.

As for the budget and learning to live within our means...all we both knew about a budget was when it came time to rent a car.

I think making the decision to have children should be part of the "Life's Plan" right from the beginning in the marriage. If you got the where for all to make the decision to get married, certainly somewhere along the way you both are going to look at each other and ask the question....

Well honey, what are we going to do with our lives?

To be sure I am grateful for the children. I don't know what I would do without them. It is bad enough to be alone at this stage of the game. Being alone without them to talk to and see would be tough.

If you haven't figured it out by now, I didn't do such a good job with my "Life's Plan" until later on in life. I am living proof that it is never too late to get with the plan.

I am no Doc. Smock. I don't have a clue but what my experience as a father has taught me. I was mostly in their early years an absentee father, even before the divorce. I regret that immensely.

That is why I think; no, I know it is so paramount that couples before they even get married start to communicate on what their expectations are of the future. If they will put as much effort into discussing the future as they do in planning their marriage and honeymoon they got a jump on life, right from the beginning.

There must be an end game. You just can't go thru life without a plan and expect much to be accomplished. Having children is a huge part of that plan.

Getting "Free" is still what this is all about. Time goes by so fast that before you know it, the kids are married and wondering what they are going to be doing with their lives. As a couple if you have set specific goals in your "Life's Plan"; set an example of living within or below your means, then chances are your children are going to know exactly what is going to become of their lives.

They are going to plan and end up "Free" just like their parents.

55. CHANCES ARE WHAT EVER IT IS YOU THINK RIGHT NOW IS A BIG DEAL, IN A SHORT PERIOD OF TIME IT WON'T MAKE ANY DIFFERENCE.

From the outside looking at almost every single marriage or relationship, they can look nice and rosy most of the time. That is not the case in most marriages. Turmoil of some kind normally abounds in most marriages and relationships. That turmoil more than likely stems from financial issues. That is not all the time and I realize that. But let's face it…the financial condition of anybody, married, single or in a relationship is the number one thing that is at issue. It is a daily challenge in all our lives.

Disagreements come and go. Assuming they don't have to do with infidelity. Dealing with financial issues is every month, every week, every day, every hour, every minute right down to the seconds. It is a stress that never goes away. It is an Irma all over again and she never goes away. Unless. It doesn't exist.

How can it not exist? If there is enough money there isn't going to be any financial issues. I do admit, even when there is enough money, people tend to find something to make a big deal out of. But, once again, if there is enough money, then there isn't going to be financial issues to deal with.

It doesn't make any difference how much your income is, individually or combined. If you are combining funds or living on one source of income, or even living off the income of a business, there is or there isn't enough money.

It isn't the amount of money that is available, unless there is none. It is all about where you allocate it and how you spend it. But you aren't going to know anything until you find out where you are spending your money. Do the budget. Then do the "Life's Plan."

Then execute both.

If you are fighting over money or anything else, what seems like a big deal right now, a day, a week or a month for now, and for sure a year from now you won't remember what it is. The big deals yes. If you live in San Francisco or close and you just got home and found your wife in bed with the quarterback for the 49'er football team that might be construed as a big deal. Particularly if he has already placed money on the night stand.

But if you just got home with your weekly paystub and you know there isn't going to be enough money to make it until next week that is not a big deal. It is time to say I am through living like this. It is a reason for action.

It is time to go into the bathroom again, shut the door, look at yourself in the mirror, again and say…"OK. Enough is enough. When she gets home we are going to sit down and talk about this and get started."

It is as close to insanity as it can be for anybody to keep doing the same thing over and over and over again with the same bad results.

56. YOU MUST HAVE A HEALTHY COMMUNICATION.

If you are not talking to each other than just grunts, then things probably need to start changing. You are in this and are part of it so why not do the best you can?

If you are ignoring things, don't want to deal with them, are a procrastinator, are fearful the way they may come out or just don't care, then surely you can't expect things to be very good in your marriage. You, the marriage and everything else you are doing and involved in are probably going to fail.

Why self destruct? Why not take charge and own it all? Take responsibility. Start communicating and have weekly meetings with your spouse on where things are in the relationship and lord knows, it just isn't going to be a discussion about money. The timing of these meetings and discussions are as important as what you discuss. When you are having dinner or breakfast is not a good time. Before going to work and immediately getting home after work is also not the time. If there are kids, they should be occupied or even better out of the house or at grandpa and grandmas. It should be when both of you are fresh, alert and engaged.

Weekends one would think would be the best time and not at the end of the weekend but the beginning of the weekend. They should be positive and not confrontational. If you have a budget and a "Life's Plan" you are involved in, then you already have an outline of what you are going to discuss.

It should center on how to make everything better. Not about where you failed to accomplish the past weeks goals. There should be no finger pointing but admitting "I can do better." We can do better. We all can do better at anything if we just put our minds to it.

There is nothing bad going to come out of this kind of communication. I am certainly not talking about having a conversation during the meeting about who is going to win the Super Bowl. Who gives a shit? What you both need to care about and concentrate on is acknowledging your achievements and rewarding yourself with…if nothing else a big hug.

You have these meetings regularly and it isn't going to be long and the results will be overwhelming. If you are single and you have jumped into the "Life's Plan" with both feet, having this meeting weekly with yourself obviously becomes a different set of circumstances. But it is just as important as if there is a husband, a wife or a significant other involved.

You want things to go south quick. Then just keep doing what you are doing. You will continue to be part of the seven or eight out of ten couples in this country that live paycheck to paycheck.

Keep doing it the way you are, and you will never get to experience the feeling of being "Free" and "Telling the World to Kiss Your Ass."

57. BOTH OF YOU MUST HAVE THE SAME VISION OF SUCCESS AND AGREE ON THE DEFINITION OF SUCCESS.

This is probably a tough one for couples. If there is only you defining what success is and working towards that definition as a goal, it is a lot easier by yourself.

But if there are two of you coming up with what the definition of success is, then it could and probably will be more complicated. Doesn't need to be, it is called communicating. It is the same with the definition of "Free." You must agree with one another. Or it is all going to be just one big waste of time.

Once you both see success from the same perspective and have put those ideals within the context of you're "Life's Plan." Then it is just a matter of executing. The budget is the same. It doesn't need to be made difficult. Difficult takes the fun out of the process.

Besides, keep one thing in mind. Nothing lasts forever. So what if one of you must "give in" and the other has to say "Ok" I can do that. I will commit to that.

This isn't about one or the other person getting their way. This isn't about punishing one person because their spending habits aren't quite what they should be. This isn't about making the other person feel inferior and not part of the relationship. This is about both of you getting "Free." This is about getting into a position in life, in the not too far distant future and having some choices in life. Right now, you don't have any choices but to keep working and keep paying and keep living from pay check to pay check.

Even if you aren't living from paycheck to paycheck chances are there is a lot of improvement you can still make in the relationship. It should be a work in process and you must be willing to adapt. Not just one member of the marriage or relationship. But both of you.

There surely can't be anything more rewarding then after a couple of years, looking back at where you were from a financial standpoint and where you are now. You may still have some debt to pay off. But you should have money in the savings account and your investment portfolio is growing. You have lived by your standards and have lived up to your commitments.

You go in the bathroom and look at the person you knew you could become, and you are proud of that person.

That is huge.

58. YOU BOTH NEED A POSITIVE OUTLOOK ON LIFE

It is tough to maintain a positive outlook on life with floods, fires, hurricanes, volcanoes, earthquakes, deaths, miscarriages, cars breaking down, losing jobs, parents passing away, dead batteries, flat tires, bills to pay, not enough money, no vacations and the pressures of life as they are today.

To maintain that positive outlook is tough enough for one individual. But when there are two involved it becomes a never-ending challenge. When one of the partners in the marriage/relationship maintains a positive outlook no matter what and the other one has a negative outlook on things that happen, it becomes impossible.

What would be nice if we all knew exactly how things were going to be before we made the decision to get married? I don't know of any marriage that doesn't change when the dust settles after the first couple of years.

Life is what it is. I do believe that are things that you can control with practicing the five P's constantly.

The five P's you say?

Proper Preparation Prevents Poor Performance.

But what life brings into the marriage or relationship in the way of Mother's Natures way of doing things, God's way of doing things and the Devil's way of doing things, we have no control. One minute the house and all the belongings are there and the next minute they are gone in a raging wild fire. Including the two cars that you just paid off and didn't put comprehensive insurance on them. Nothing is left. It is very difficult to maintain a positive outlook on life when that happens. One minute 16-month-old Brad is playing in the back yard and the next minute he is gone. Drowned in a ditch in less than five minutes. It happens.

One day you go to work, and you are home by noon. Your job for the last 16 years has been terminated because of a corporate merger. It happens. If you don't have a spouse that has a positive outlook and a can-do attitude and can't accept "It is what it is" then there is going to be hell to be paid. It is going to take a lot of work to save that marriage and get back on track.

I maintain that it is life itself that must be managed, con-stantly. Hence the "Life's Plan." If you are prepared, know you have stayed true to each other and are executing that plan you both came up with, then no matter what happens, you can keep moving forward.

Getting attached to "stuff" is a mistake from my experiences. The less you have, the less you must pack, the less you must move and the less you must replace. The less you have the less you must sell, give away or throw away. The less you have, means the less money you have spent and the more you saved.

Getting from point A to point R is going to take a lot of work, commitment and sacrifice and planning. But the sooner you get there than the sooner you can "Tell the World to Kiss Your Ass."

Nobody knows where your "there" is but you two. That is the way it should be.

Imagine this? You both have been working your "Life's Plan" now for 22 years. You have achieved the goals of financial security and the other meaningful aspects of the "Life's Plan." You invite all your friends over for a Saturday afternoon barbecue and once everyone is there, you announce the following:

You both have resigned from your jobs. The three kids are out of the house and on their own. Everything you have is paid for including the house. You have more than $1.4 million in cash, investments and interest-bearing accounts. You are going to sell the house and go travel for two years, then decide during that two-year period where you are going to live and continue to fulfill your "Life's Plan."

Both of you are thinking that you want to buy a B & B somewhere in Western Montana, not far from Glacier National Park, perhaps around Whitefish, Montana. However, you also want to start to experience the retirement aspect of the change. Spending time together and learning to live with the changes and make sure you don't make the wrong decisions.

It doesn't make any difference what the decision is if you make sure it is the right one. And make it together. You can always make a change later. That is what is great about being able to "Tell the World to Kiss Your Ass." You can do anything you want. Go anywhere you want.

If you stay true to the five P's and stay committed to the "Life's Plan" you are in 100% control.

Start to make plans on what you are going to tell your friends at your barbecue. What you tell them will come directly out of the results of the "Life's Plan."

It will never happen if you both don't have compatibility in maintaining a very positive outlook on life, no matter what comes your way.

59. YOU MUST TRUST EACH OTHER.

Can anyone tell me something that is more important in a marriage or a relationship than trusting each other? Unequivocally. Of course, that trust must be going both ways. If there becomes any doubt in a marriage or a relationship, when it comes to trusting the other, by either one of the partners… than the relationship is broken. Nothing can be more troubling than going to work day in and day out and wondering if you can trust your spouse or significant other. Nothing.

That trust must be all encompassing.

Particularly when it comes to staying true. It means not straying into the pasture full of heifers or bulls. It also means trusting one another when it comes to financial issues.

Initially, financial issues are probably the most common thing couples fight over. It usually means there isn't enough money to go around. If there is enough, then the fighting is going to be over how it is spent, or more importantly how it was spent. Nothing makes for anger and resentment than knowing Johnny spent a ton of money in Las Vegas when he was on a week's convention meeting. Or, Betty spent way too much time at the mall in Macy's. Money spent like that just can't be redeemed most of the time. Sure, Betty could take the stuff back. Then she is really going to have some resentment.

Johnny has a hard time explaining where $3,700 went. Especially when the company was paying for the air fare, the hotels and the meals. Tough situation.

None of these kinds of things would be an issue at all if there was a commitment to the "Life's Plan." Neither Johnny nor Betty would even think of spending any money in any amount without a consultation with the other. A discussion and a meeting of the minds. The urge would not even be there. In the beginning when the budget and the "Life's Plan" were put into place and executed, it has become a good habit that neither strays. That sort of thing just won't happen.

Without the budget and the "Life's Plan" then it is easily spent in Vegas and at Macy's. Another month goes by living from paycheck to paycheck.

Being true to your spouse or your partner is one thing. But being true to yourself is a completely different set of circumstances. You will never accomplish much of anything if you aren't true to yourself. That means making commitments and living up to them. That means telling somebody you are going to do something and doing it.

It means telling your spouse or partner that you will live up to the budget and to the "Life's Plan" and doing so. It means success or failure.

It means doing it together.

You must find a level of trust that is uncommon.

60. FIND SIMPLE

Simple is, simple does. Who said that? It is hard to find simple these days. Everything is so complicated, computerized and made difficult to do or understand. The younger generation doesn't even notice how difficult their lives are. They probably never well. But simple in my opinion is where it all makes a difference.

Does it really take all that we have or want or end up with to lead a "happy, joyous and free" life? Yes, I know… I am old, older and tired of the rat race but let's face it, simple makes sense.

Life is tough enough as it is without coming up with ways to make it more difficult. There are many, many ways a couple can come up with doing things in such way that simplifies their lives.

One of the most obvious is to have money. You can earn it by working. It can be given to you in an inheritance. You win the Lottery. Or you are good at Day Trading. I don't care where it comes from. But you must have it. Making money is easy if you apply yourself. Ending up with some of it is an entirely different set of circumstances.

The easiest way to simplify your life or lives is to do the budget. Then sit down and outline the "Life's Plan." Then perfect the "Life's Plan" and then start to execute it. Once you start seeing the little successes, which are almost imme-diately, then as time goes by the simple part of the entire process unfolds. It gets easier and easier and easier.

Before long…life becomes simple. There is enough money. You are eliminating your debt. You are in 100% control. You have choices. You see the results everywhere in your lives. It becomes fun. The success of it all starts to feel like you are being rewarded. Which you are.

There will always be challenges. But those challenges are faced down with a confidence in the fact that you have achieved so much.

Doesn't make any difference what the challenges are; they too shall pass.

They always do.

61. YOU CERTAINLY DON'T NEED TO SPEND ALL YOUR TIME TOGETHER.

Marriage and/or relationships, in my experience doesn't mean either one of you must lose your independence. Being able to spend time away from each other is a good way to maintain that independence. Finding endeavors to do on your own, as well as together helps to nourish and makes the marriage and/or relationship just that much stronger.

Going on vacations together, the kid's athletic events, concerts, business trips, doing the yard work and the honey dos on the weekend together should just come naturally one would hope.

But going on separate vacations, going on retreats, business trips separately also is a good way to get away from each other and get that always welcomed break. If the woman in the marriage and/or relationship is a stay at home mom, then that becomes a whole set of different circumstances. However, there are always ways to make things work when it comes to getting away together and/or individually.

If you have your "Life's Plan" before you and you are living and breathing it, you are in 100% control. Maintaining living within or below the budget you both have set before you also allows you to make choices.

The "Life's Plan" and the success of the budget just makes it all that much easier to do things individually and together. You have the money. You have the experience of planning. You have confidence and more importantly you are having fun. You have eliminated a tremendous amount of stress in your lives.

It certainly helps if you both have something in common. My experience from living it first hand is if you don't have some things in common right from the beginning, chances are you aren't going to be able to create that kind of relationship where you do everything together.

You don't go out and start climbing mountains because your partner does. You may have never even seen a mountain.

You aren't going to find the desire to do a 100-day kayak trip, only getting a shower a couple of times during that 100 days if you think a kayak is a ship. That just doesn't work and it never well. That is why I believe it is important that before it all consummates into "I Do", it would probably be a wise decision to know you have things in common. Look beyond the stars in your eyes. Go climb a mountain together or do a 30-day kayak trip together. That ought to give each of you something to think about.

At some point in time it all becomes common sense. Decisions are driven by experiences that you have yourself, or you can look at other people's experiences and see yourself.

Reality has a way of being the only bench mark to live by. You can wish and want all you can.

But it will come down to the fact,

"It is what it is."

CHAPTER SIX: PLAY

62. FIND WHAT MAKES YOU WANT TO DO IT AGAIN, THEN KEEP DOING IT.

We are not talking about sex here. I have got to the point in life where sex and eating are way over rated anyway. We are talking about finding something that you like to do for enjoyment.

Every one of us is different. A lot of us like to do the same things. But what I enjoy doing for fun; for relaxation, for excitement, the very thing that fulfills me is not necessarily what you are going to find that fulfills you.

It doesn't make any difference what it is. But it should be something you look forward to doing and enjoy. Finding the outlet to find joy and happiness in doing something other than work is essential. It is part of that healthy thing that makes the difference between a fulfilled life and one that is always longing to be fulfilled. In fact, it should be several things if that is you.

I kayak, river raft, paint, always working on a project to refinish/rebuild something, read, keep things clean and orga-nized, keep the yard clean, walk every day and exercise every day. There is never any down time in my life. Very seldom do I find myself looking for something to do.

The fact that there is no TV time in my life makes the difference. Once you get rid of the TV you will within days be looking around for something to do. That is when the fun kicks in. You suddenly realize what a waste of time that TV has been in your life.

More importantly, having a great variety of things to do prepares you over the years for when it comes time to quit the rat race and throw in the towel. You don't have to worry about what you are going to be doing after you "tell the world to kiss your ass" and retire. You have already been doing it for years.

You must keep reinforcing your thought processes from a positive point of view. Getting "Free" is not for free. No one is going to just come along, knock on your front door, hand you a package and that is your freedom. You must plan and work at it. You need to constantly focus and concentrate on making sure.... your "Life's Plan" is adapting to the changes in your life.

A lot of money isn't going to make it happen either. Money can make a lot of good things happen. At the same time money can make a lot of bad things happen. There is a lot more to being "Free" than having financial security. Lot of people with a lot of money are losing the game. They have no clue what it means to be "Free."

Success brings self-confidence. Self-confidence brings more success. It is that simple.

Don't make this difficult.

63. GO WALKING

It has been repeated several times up to this point that walking
on a consistent basis has done a great deal for my health and
my emotional stability. It is the number one thing in my life
that brings me constant joy. I look forward to it every morning. The days I don't go for a walk, I know it. There is just
something different about the way the days goes.

Something as simple a walking daily can help you live a
much healthier life. Regular brisk walking can help you
maintain a healthy weight. It can help prevent or manage
various conditions, including high blood pressure, type two
diabetes and heart disease. It helps strengthen your bones
and muscles. Walking improves your mood, balance and
coordination.

Walking and exercise can possibly buy you two to six years
more on your life. But if you are 87 and healthy it means a
lot. The great part about what makes walking so beneficial is
that when you're walking you can't be sitting. There is that
throw the TV thing out again.

Somewhere I read where research showed that getting up
and walking around for two minutes out of every hour can
increase your life's span by 33% compared to those that
don't. Say that again? 33%? We spend somewhere between
nine to ten hours a day sitting. That doesn't include the
couch in the evenings and on the weekends. The average

person walks only between 3,000 and 4,000 steps per day and it should be more than 10,000. I suppose you could walk around the couch while the TV is blaring.

Walking burns the same number of calories as running. It just takes longer. When you see the true runner; he or she is just working harder and beating the hell out of him or herself to achieve the same results you can get by just going for a good…long walk.

You will never get to the point of getting to the "Free Spot" if you don't make this walking thing a part of your "Life's Plan." By sharing my life's experiences, good or bad, right or wrong, the successes and the failures, it is all about getting "Free." Getting to the point of having complete and total control of your life in every aspect is nothing more than executing the plan.

The time you take to walk everyday is not a waste of time. You can think. You can clear your thought processes. You can plan, and you can visualize yourself telling everyone when the time comes to "kiss your ass."

Folks. There is nothing better than being in that position. Just look around you.

What you see just isn't that pretty of a picture.

You don't have to be part of that picture.

64. GO HIKING

If this book gets read at all, a lot of folks are probably thinking this guy is nuts. For sure he is eccentric and somewhat
off the wall. Maybe.

But from my perspective it is a good thing. Nature is good.
Nature is nurturing. Nature can solve a lot of problems.
It can generate a lot of goodness in one's life. That is why
you see me referring to so many things that require being
outside. The sun is good. Too much sun is not so good.
But there are ways to mitigate too much sun.

I don't think one time throughout this entire book have I
even remotely referred to being inside for any reason, for any
length of time.

I hate being inside.

Hiking is one of those ways to connect or re-connect for that
matter with oneself. You don't have to go hiking alone to have
that happen. I don't care where you live in this country going
hiking is no more than a day's drive or less from any large metropolitan area. Going hiking when you live in an area where
it is only a 30-minute drive is easily planned and executed.

It doesn't cost a lot of money to get the gear together necessary to take a safe hike. Whether it is for a day or a week,
gear is easily available. There are many 2nd hand/or resell
stores that sell used sports, camping and hiking equipment.

There is no better way to get away from the hustle and bustle of life than going hiking and sleep under the stars or in a tent. Hiking up and down hills on a trail is exhilarating and great for your emotional and physical health. There is just something good about cooking your meals over a campfire or a small camp stove that just seems to make it all taste better.

There is also no better way for a relationship to reconnect than spending some time together. Just the two of you when you are hiking. There is a lot of time that affords the kind of conversations you just don't seem to have or take the time to have when life is all around you.

It is the birds singing that stirs my soul. It is my way of connecting with my higher power. It is the way I give thanks for my health and for what I am grateful for in life. When I am paddling down the river, on a lake or hiking on a trail is when I am the most grounded. The most connected. The most centered.

Go take a hike.

65. GO CAMPING.

Is camping the same thing as hiking? No, it isn't. You can be camping while you are hiking every night. But going for a camping trip by yourself, with your significant other or your family is a whole different experience. Places to go camping are endless; I don't care where you live in the country. There are places you can go camping with 1,000 other people or you can find place to go camping where there is a good chance there won't be anybody. When I am on one of my kayak trips…if there is one other person on the river within 100 miles that is one person to many for me.

Like hiking, camping is a connection with being outdoors. It is the nature thing again that makes it all worth it. It doesn't have to cost a lot of money. If you have done your "Life's Plan" correctly and have achieved your goals on dictating your budget, you have put plenty of monies in the budget for what it cost to go camping whenever you want to.

You don't need a $100,000-dollar Class A Motor Home to go camping. You don't need a Motor Home period. What you do need is some good camping gear, a good sense of safety and a desire to experience life without all the stress, hustle and bustle of day to day living.

When you do go, and I hope you do, make sure it is somewhere where you can hear nature. Don't take the TV if you haven't got rid of it yet. Don't take the laptop. Don't take your notebook. Don't take your iPod. Don't take your Go Pro. Don't take the Drone. Don't take the camera. Do take your phone for emergencies. But try not to look at it until you get in your rig to head home.

When you get all set up, just sit down and listen.

Go camping next weekend.

66. PLAY AS HARD OR HARDER THAN YOU WORK

From an early age in life we are conditioned to work. We watch our parents go to work. We watch the neighbors go to work. Everyone grows up watching their sphere of influence go to work. Then one day it comes our turn. Whether it is the paper route, mowing lawns, raking leaves, baby sitting, most of us find a job in high school. Or we use to.

Then we graduate high school and we work summers while going to college. Or a lot of students work while they are going to college. Or some of us join the service, which is a form of work. A lot of young people just go to work right after high school. They don't go to college or join the service. I have a feeling a lot of young people don't work, got to college, or join the service these days. I am not sure what they do.

Regardless, at some point in time most of us end up going to work. Day after day just like all those adults we saw going to work as we were growing up. Not much changes. What changes is the attitude toward work. I just read another article about 80% of the work force in this country lives from pay check to pay check. Right there is another reason you go to work. You have to.

But think about this? What if you didn't have to? Didn't have to what? Go to work! You just need to spend a little bit more time in the bathroom and visualize the $1.5 million in the savings and portfolio. Then you must visualize yourself giving your two-week notice at work. It is not out of the question for this to happen. You just make it happen.

Apart from work there is this play thing. The play thing can include all kinds of activities that don't include the idea of work. I am not going to go thru the umpteen things you can do when it comes to playing. I consider piddling, working at something playing. I always have. I refer to it as "going fishing."

The difference between your attitude towards working and playing I believe centers around this one fact.

Do you have to, or do you do it because you want to?

OK. $1.5 million seems to be a little bit too much in your mind's eye. Then let's go once again into the bathroom and visualize $1 million. Everyone seems to like to throw that figure around these days. Depending on what age you are when you start your "Life's Plan", then perhaps a million is more realistic. But if you start this ball rolling in your mid to late 20's, $1.5 million is very doable. Which means starting to play…retire in your 50's is more than possible.

You got to play hard in my opinion or don't play at all. No different than your working. You want to work hard, diligently, smart and live up to your commitment. Or find something else you can commit to and work hard at it. It must be the same thing when it comes to playing. Doesn't make any difference what it is. Do it well. Do it often. Put your heart and soul in to it.

By doing this, you become accustomed to working hard, playing hard and above all you are 150% committed to your "Life's Plan" and living within your budget.

What a zoo things are turning out to be these days. What a stressor to even mildly try to keep up with all the turmoil. One of the main reasons I don't watch TV, read the periodicals, read the newspapers is because all of it is just horseshit anyway.

There are many, many ways one can contribute to this country above and beyond participating in all the horseshit.

One of the best ways in my opinion is to be honest, do right, help others and don't become part of the problem. Work at becoming part of the solution no matter how trivial your contribution may seem.

Another way is to maintain a life that centers on being "Happy, Joyous and Free" and play, play, play.

67. GO KAYAKING, CANOEING, BIKE RIDING

Somebody right now, if I have been lucky enough to sell a copy of this book, is probably saying "is this guy ever going to get off the outdoor stuff." Nope. Outdoors is all I know. I don't even like sleeping indoors if I can get away with it.

Now I know a lot of people live in very large metropolitan areas and the idea of "outdoors" is almost impossible. Don't know what to tell you. I can't relate to it. I have spent time in Los Angeles, San Diego, Anchorage, Portland, OR and other populated areas. Never again. My only advice is get out and get out as soon as you can. You say....easy to say but impossible to do.

Perhaps. It is all a matter of choice.

What I am trying to focus on is the path to achieving your "Life's Plan." I believe that needs to be a balanced approach. It will be a lot of work and play with a commitment to the "Life's Plan" in between. You can call it sacrifice if you want to. I like to call it commitment.

Kayaking, canoeing, bike riding, horseback riding, walking, cross country skiing, skiing, camping, hiking, kite flying the choices are endless. It needs to be something. It must be something. If all you are doing is watching TV, looking at the phone, gaming and saving enough money for the next tattoo, you are on a road to despair. There will be winners and there will be losers. The losers are obvious. Most of the winners are recognizable over a given period. A loser can become a winner. A winner can turn into a loser. I have been both.

I have found that by focusing on my health with outdoor activities I have transgressed from a loser at times to a winner all the time. Fortunately, I have, for myself, defined what I believe to be the definition of a winner.

68. LEARN TO PAINT

This one will be short and to the point. I didn't get on to painting until after I was 70. I needed to find something else to do in the evenings. The worst time of the day for me is 5PM plus or minus to 8PM plus or minus. This challenge during this part of the day is a result of the no TV thing. I can just read so much and limit it because I believe reading can lead to being sedentary.

My daughter Chrissi paints/draws at times. I saw a painting of a flower she painted, and I thought to myself; I can do that.

A trip to Hobby Lobby and couple hundred dollars later I was set up to try my hand at painting. Surprisingly enough, what I painted to begin with looks like what I wanted it to. In fact, the 1st painting I did is the one so far, I am most proud of.

Painting has motivated me once again to do something different. That "New View" thing I advocate. I enjoy it immensely and of course there is no shortage of what to paint.

The painting doesn't have to be perfect. Getting it perfect is not what I set out to do. What I set out to do was to continue to fulfill my "Life's Plan." The part of the plan that ensures I stay active, busy, motivated and above all focused on having a fulfilled and productive life. Your plan should never end. But it must change with the times.

It does not have to be painting. But it does have to be something.

69. LEARN TO PLAY A MUSICAL INSTRUMENT

Not everybody is musical inclined. You don't have to be to get benefit out of learning to play some music. I started 1st with the Native Flute. It isn't perfected yet to the point I can step out on the stage, but I do have fun with it at times.

I am inclined towards the piano and have been practicing now for some time. I am not even close to where I wish I was. But once again that is not the point. It is the doing. It is the new thing. It is the fact that once again I am trying to fulfill the need to keep moving down the road and not get stuck in a pot hole. I wished I would have started the piano years ago. I wanted to but never did. Shame on me. It was a mistake. But I am trying to make up for it.

You don't have to wait until you are "Free." In fact, I wish a lot of what I do today, and it is a lot compared to others, I would have started the process and had it in my "Life's Plan" years ago. I failed to focus on what was important to my well being and only did what I knew and was used to. Most of the time those things were a waste of time, money and emotional capital. That is the challenge for most of us. Breaking out of the mold. Jumping the fence to the other side. Deciding that things need to change. How someone can look out their front window and see the same view for 60 years is beyond me.

Once again, it is all a matter of choice.

CHAPTER SEVEN: FINANCIAL

70. IF YOU DON'T OWE ANY MONEY… YOU ARE "FREE."

Credit. It is taught in kindergarten to be the greatest thing in the world. Without credit you are a nobody. I know a lady who thinks having ten credit cards in her wallet, all maxed out is the sure sign of being successful.

If you don't have a credit score by the time you are 12, then you are a failure. Get a car for zero down and 72 months of payments is also the sign of being successful. If you have a paycheck you can get a car loan. Interest rate probably will be 18%, but who cares. It is the zero down that gets you.

Problem is these payments go on for ever and ever and ever. If course no one at your insurance company offered you "Gap Insurance" so you wreck the car and find out, you owe $8,000 dollars on the car more than the insurance company will pay for totally the car. Oh, and the dealer forgot to tell you that your new $37,000 car will only be worth $17,000 a month after you drive it off the lot.

You must have a credit card. All your friends do. You just aren't one of the crowd without it. In fact, three cards are better than just having one.

What happens here is as you start to get into your early teens and for sure into your early 20's you are in debt. To compound the problem, you probably also have about $80,000 in student loan debt to pay off if you do in fact graduate from college. You start your life out, when you finally get to work, in debt up to your ass.

That starts the vicious cycle of working what they call "For the Man." You get your paycheck, sit down at the kitchen table with your new honey and baby and give it all to somebody else. Week after week, month after month, year after year this is what you do.

If you make enough, then you get a mortgage, and probably a 30-year mortgage on that new house. A 30-year mortgage is a license for the banks and mortgage companies to steal. Once again, you sit down at the kitchen table with your pay check, little older honey by now and three kids looking on and you give all your pay check to somebody else. You can't even take the kids to a movie and if you do you put it on the credit card that has only a couple hundred dollars left on it.

This vicious cycle goes on and on. Week after week, month after month, year after year. It is normal. It is what you were taught. It is what the system likes and works awful hard to keep you doing.

Give it up. Get out of debt. No matter how. No matter what it takes. Start over. No credit cards. No charging of any kind. No eating out. No new cars. Try not buying anything new for a year. Get the student loans paid off.

The definition of "Free" can mean a lot of things. But the only definition of "Free" that means everything, is "Debt Free."

71. SAVE 20% OF EVERY GROSS DOLLAR YOU MAKE.

This 20% is on your gross income, not after taxes. Why? Because it makes a huge difference in the long run. Or short run for that matter. I am not going to do the math for you. But it is all a matter of budgeting. Making commitments. Sticking to those commitments no matter what. Living below your means.

No matter how much you are making it is doable. For instance. No TV. No going out to eat. Bare minimum cell bill. No vehicle. Or only one vehicle. Better yet, two paid for if you need two. Ride the bus. Ride your bike. No Starbucks or the like. No ballgames. No basketball games. No vacations. It is called sacrifice. It is called commitment. It isn't forever. Nothing lasts forever. Nothing.

Maybe because of circumstances only 5% at first can be achieved. It makes no difference who you are, how old you are, married or single, how many kids you have, you invariably and consistently piss away and waste 30% or more of your expendable income. Probably more unless you are at minimum wage or perhaps a little higher.

For one month keep track of every penny you spend. It makes no difference if it is $2,000 per month or $20,000 per month. Keep track of every penny and it will astound you how much you waste and can save.

Get rid of the car payments, credit cards and for sure the charge cards. Close your Amazon account. Close them all.

What do you do with the money you save? I have a few suggestions. So, would everyone else.

I met a guy out riding his wave runner on Lake Havasu a couple of months ago while I was paddling my kayak. As usual the conversation eventually ended up with us talking about being "Free." Being able to live our life financially secure. Doing what we wanted to. He told me that the best advice he ever got was from a classmate of his when he started college. His classmate's father worked for Edward Jones. His friend told him if there was nothing else he ever did, the best thing to do right now was walk into the nearest Edward Jones office and start a plan for retirement. He did. He retired out of the Anchorage, AK police department after 24 years with a whole lot of money invested and owns everything he has. He was 54. That is a great example of a successful "Life's Plan."

Whatever you decide it must be a vehicle to compounding the growth of the money and 100% secure. Once you achieve your "Life's Plan" goal then you can invest a small percentage of it in the stock market. Go to Las Vegas. Invest in the hotel you brother-in-law is building. But only after you have got to the point of telling everyone and the world you are "Free", and "the world can kiss your ass."

I am not advocating not enjoying life and only hoarding money. You want more money. Create multiple streams of income. Start a homebased business. Sell chicken eggs.

Quit wasting money. Get yourself in a position to finding a higher paying job. Think and make good common-sense decisions as you adapt and change your "Life's Plan."

You have got to get serious.

Now. Immediately. Time is pushing on. You are going to be 55 or 65 or 75… like tomorrow… that is how fast it happens.

Then it is too late.

72. ORGANIZE YOUR FINANCES.

Most people sit around and watch TV, or on a bar stool or doing nothing. They spend more time staring into the refrigerator than they do thinking about their financial future.

Sit down and do a budget. As you work towards creating a "Life's Plan" it will become your number one priority. You don't need am MBA or Doctorate in accounting to be good at doing this.

It takes a pen or pencil and a yellow or legal pad. You put down your net income, after taxes. Then you take 10% or 20% of your gross income and you subtract that from your net income.

On the left, you make a list of all your monthly obligations. Only what you must pay. To the right you put the amount on each line. Then the total. Subtract that from what your monies left after saving the 20%. 20% of your gross not your net. It is very, very simple.

Then you make another list of all the necessities. Food, medicine, school lunches, gas, vehicle maintenance, parking fees, so on and so forth. The list can be endless and normally is. Add it all up and deduct it from the balance of your monies left after the "have to pay." The money left is probably going to Starbucks, cigars, cigarettes, pot, beer, wine, whiskey, dinners out, expenditures you "DON'T HAVE TO

MAKE." But you do, day in and day out.

Unless you are a very rare individual or couple, you don't have enough money. Hence the credit cards.

Now go for a walk with me on this. To even have a clue where all your money is going after the "have to pay list" you must keep track for at least a month on where your money is going. Should be six months. Every penny. Doing a budget is senseless and meaningless until you have this information. It will make you sick to find out just how much money you waste.

Here we go again. If you aren't getting up every morning and practicing the "5 P's." Then you in my opinion are pissing in the wind. If you really want to ever get to the point you can and do "tell the world to kiss your ass" you should be working at executing the "5 P's" every waking hour.

Proper Preparation Prevents Poor Performance.

It is called control. Being centered. Grounded. In the zone. Spot on.

Doing this exercise in creating a budget is nothing more than you are working towards your "Life's Plan." It should be visited every single day when you get started. Then once a week make sure your financial resources are going where you said you would put them.

Here is the most important thing I have learned concerning all of this. If I tell myself I am going to do something, and I don't do it then I have let myself down. Letting somebody else down is bad enough. Letting yourself down is the worst of all. It becomes a very bad habit.

Making a budget, a plan on how you or you and your family are going to spend those hard-earned dollars is a test in how honest, truthful and committed you can be to yourself.

73. DEMAND YOUR MONEY'S WORTH.

When I was a kid, I remember my Dad commenting on he was going to work hard in his business. He was going to give his customer's their "Money's Worth." Therefore, he expected the same from those where he spent his money.

Probably wasn't a common occurrence in those days when you didn't get your money's worth. Today it is the norm. From cheap goods. Too bad food. To new vehicles that are lemons. Too bad tires. To crap in the box. To poor workmanship. To poor customer service. Have you bought a new RV lately? There's crap to a T. A candy bar that is half the size it used to be. An energy bar that is barely enough for a mouse to get any energy/protein out of. Everywhere you spend your money it is prevalent.

I don't spend a lot of money any more except on the necessities. Anymore I try not to buy much of anything that can't go in one end and come out the other.

I got some bad gas on a trip recently traveling thru the desert. I almost didn't make it to the next gas which solved the problem. Who do you go to and complain? Get your money back. You just have to accept it. That is pretty much the best analogy you can get when it comes to trying to get your money's worth in every single situation you are spending it. You just have to accept it.

One must be constantly aware of where your money is going. Where it is about to go. Can you get a better price down the street? On another website? Are there hidden costs? How in the world can a breakfast in Napa, CA cost $82.00 for 2 people?

Plane tickets are another mystery. One day the flight you want to take is $124. The next day it is $324. To the same place, the same day at the same time.

Food is a cost to all of us that is difficult to manage. But it can be if you want to take the time. You don't have to go to Whole Foods or a boutique store to get good wholesome food.

I thought I would never say something like this. But I find myself going to WalMart more and more. That is by no means a plug for WalMart, but they make it easy. Financially less painful. I seem to walk out the door with what I wanted. With what I only need and spending less.

I don't care how much money you have. It is a bad habit to just spend with no cost controls. No direction. No list and no mission in mind.

You must work very hard at getting your money's worth these days. Folks, it ain't going to get any easier. So, the sooner you get with it the sooner you are on your way to being "Free."

74. DO NOT BANK WITH A BANK.

Not too many days go by where we read or hear from the
system that another bank has agreed to pay another fine in
the millions for their shady dealings and dishonest banking
practices? For me I think it has been two days. I flat out
hate banks. Next to credit card companies, thieves, swin-
dlers, con artists and the likes, banks are deceitful through
and through. Credit Unions are fast coming up on the inside, but at least they aren't as bad. Yet. But they are getting
there.

I am not assuming what I just articulated. It is a fact and
is proved routinely and constantly. But they are still stay
in business, making money and it is lots of money. Why
is that? That is because they prey on the uneducated. The
unassuming. The foreigner. The down trodden. The broke.
People who watch too much TV.

All of them are the same. Yes, I admit it, there are people
aware and know what they are doing and bank with them. I
don't understand why.

It is simple when it comes to the individual. You have a
choice and that choice is to not do business with them.
They churn customers amongst themselves like a dairy farm-
ers wife use to churn butter in the old days.

Move your banking to a Credit Union. They still have over

draft fees. They still must build new branches. Replace lawns out front and have monthly fees. They must make enough to pay for the cost of doing business. But they operate differently and have you, their customer's best interest in mind. Most of the time.

You still must be aware of what you are doing. What kind of account you have and what it is costing you. A Credit Union is different. It is a better business and banking decision to manage your money in their system.

Make no mistake about it, it is a fact and always will be the traditional big banking system is fraught with fraud, deceit and thievery. For those of you that might happen to work for a big bank and you are reading this book. I am not throwing you under the bus. I know you need a job. But if I were you, for the sake of your soul and a good night's sleep.

Find another job.

75. IF YOU HAVE TO FILE BANKRUPTCY, DO SO.

You are in debt in every way possible. Credit cards. Vehicle loans. Behind in the rent or mortgage payment. You owe state and federal income taxes. Medical bills. You household monthly bills. You name it, you owe it and no way can you pay it. It happens all the time. You are not the first person or couple or family to get into debt. They make it easy to get into debt. They also make it easy to get out of debt.

What I am about to expound upon is only my opinion. What I say is based on a whole lot of experience from being in debt. The first thing you do is stop paying everybody now. Today. This very minute. Only pay for what it takes to put a roof over your head or you and your family. Make sure you and your family can eat. The car payments for now to get back and forth to work. The house if you have a mortgage on it, is just that, a house. Quit paying the mortgage payment and start looking for a place to rent. That's it. Don't pay anybody else. Don't worry about your credit or your FICO score. It is probably already in the tank. Right where it should be. No credit or a low FICO score means you are dead in the water on credit and that is exactly what you want.

Get all your bills together. Make a list of what must be paid and what you don't have to pay.

Go get a Chapter 7 Bankruptcy Filing Kit from one of the

stationary stores. Fill it out. Go to the closest Federal Court House and file the Chapter 7. You don't even have to pay for the filing fee if you don't have the money; they will string it out over time. You don't need an attorney. Once you file and your creditors are notified. That is it. They can't contact you anymore and they can't come after you.

Once you adjudged bankrupt in about six months you get a chance to start your life over financially. The 1st thing I would do would be to re-read this book and get started on your "Life's Plan."

Filing Bankruptcy is legal. It is a way that society has decided to give those of us a 2nd chance in learning how to manage our finances and our lives. Take an advantage of it. Be brutally honest with the system from the beginning to the end.   In two or three years you will be back to a point you can start using credit wisely and when it makes sense. In the mean time you live below your means. Within your budget. You have started saving money. You are following your "Life's Plan." Finally.

If it takes filing bankruptcy to get to this point. That is a good thing. Dave Ramsay does not think it is right to file bankruptcy. I am pretty sure on this. He believes it is the "right" thing to do to pay your debt off no matter how long it takes or how much it is. I disagree. Bankruptcy is legal, it is a way to get on the right path sooner than later and morally it is a choice of the individual.

Sounds like a good deal to me. It is. If you don't take an advantage of the system immediately, you might as well just go out and burn what money you are paying on your debt in the driveway.

Because that is exactly what you are doing when you keep paying on your debt.

Don't worry about your credit score. Don't worry about what anybody else thinks of you. Look out after yourself and your family. If it makes more sense to file bankruptcy than it does to keep paying on your debt, then that is what you should do.

Just do it. You will never regret it.

76. USE CREDIT CARDS ONLY FOR EMERGEN-CIES, CAR RENTALS AND PAY THEM OFF MONTH-LY.

Credit Card Companies are right up there with banks. A lot of the big banks are in the credit card business. That shouldn't surprise anybody. They are parasites, they are thieves and they are ruthless.

You need one credit card and it should only be for emergencies. A credit card is not to buy groceries. Make your monthly payments. Go on a vacation. They should, in my humble opinion, only be used for emergencies. Renting cars and the like. Your debit card is what you should be using.

Ah-h-h you say. But I don't have the money in my account. Therefore, I need to use the credit card to pay for that cup of coffee. My lunch. The dinner. The utility payment. The trip to Disney Land. No. If you don't have the cash to spend, then you don't have the money to spend.

Using your credit card for anything other than what you should be using it for, emergences, car rental, etc, you don't do it. You don't go there. You eat macaroni and cheese. Take the bus. Stay home. Go for a walk. Ride your bike. Do something productive that DOESN'T COST MONEY.

What is great about the credit card company's philosophy, is they make so much money, that when you get in over your head and you do file bankruptcy. It isn't but a year or two and they are sending you offers for another credit card.

When the time is right. Get one. Set the limit to $1,000 or $2,000. Use it responsibly. Pay it off at the end of the month.

If you make a lot of money, have a savings program, live within your budget, are living and breathing your "Life's Plan" using credit cards can be to your advantage. The cards that rack up the miles on the airlines are great. Everyone in a sound financial position should be utilizing these cards for everything.

Groceries, gas, making payments, taking vacations, buying the coffee, you name it, pay for it with the credit card. But you must pay the balance in full at the end of the month.

Whether it is $1,000 or $10,000 or $25,000 you must have the income, the cash flow to use a credit card this way. Business or personal. I think it is a great idea to let the credit card company pay for a lot of "free" airline tickets.

77. IF YOU BUY A HOUSE, ONLY GET A 15 YEAR MORTGAGE.

There are positives and negatives on owning a house. There are positives and negatives on renting/leasing a house. The situation for each individual and family is different.

I certainly am not going to give what I believe is a long list of positives and negatives. However, before you can own a house, you must buy a house. That means you get into the wonderful world of mortgages. Unless of course you pay cash.

Mortgages are available just about everywhere. It really doesn't make any difference where you go to get your mortgage. The qualifications everywhere you can shop for a mortgage are just about the same.

VA loans can sometimes be the easiest. You must be a veteran to be able to qualify for one. USDA home loans can also be an option, depending on your circumstances. Where you bank can be an option. But beware of the points that can be charged. Keep in mind, getting a mortgage loan is a little bit like going to a casino. Casinos, like mortgage companies exist for one simple reason. To take every single penny they can from you.

Don't be ignorant of the options for a home loan. They are vast. So are the places you can "shop" for a loan. That is exactly what you should do. Go shopping. Get the best deal you can. Then lock in the rate. Go find your house.

Here is what I believe to be a fact. Do not even consider a 30-year mortgage. 30-year mortgages are like taking your money, the amount of the loan payment, principal and interest and going out in the driveway the day it is due and burning it in a little fire. A 30-year mortgage is a license to steal.

If you can qualify for a 30-year mortgage, chances are with a little bit of additional cash for a down payment you can qualify for a 15-year mortgage.

Living under the parameters of a "Life's Plan" means you are living within your means. The difference between qualifying for a 15-year mortgage and a 30-year mortgage is not that significant. That is because after a year or two of living and breathing your "Life's Plan" you don't have any credit card payments. You don't have a vehicle payment. You don't have any retail card payments. You don't have any debt except perhaps your student loans, if you are unlucky enough to have any.

30 years is forever. 15 years is just down the road around the corner. Now think about this. Having your house paid for in 15 years is a world away from having your house paid for in 30 years. The options available to you at the end of 15 years are significantly more in number than the limited

amount of options you will have at the end of 30 years.

You want to get to the point as fast as possible to be able to

"Tell the World to Kiss Your Ass."

Having a house paid off in 15 years is going to make that happen a whole lot sooner.

78. NO CAR PAYMENTS.

Having a car payment or two or even three is right up there with no credit cards. I am very aware of how difficult it is to not have a vehicle payment. However, if I could expound upon one simple fact. That fact is not having a car payment is like winning the lottery every month. It is like getting a raise every paycheck. It is like Christmas every month. When you sit down to pay your bills. No car payment. No car payment. Say it over and over and over again. No car payment is a beautiful thing.

If you were hired by a company to go out in the entire United States and give them a number of how many good, sound, drivable vehicles under a $1,000 there was it would take you 5 life times. 10 life times. Because every day there are 1,000's and 1,000's more of them available. The numbers of those vehicles that are available are in the millions.

Go to $2,000 and below and now the number has increased significantly to in the millions and millions. If you are going back and forth to work, to school for the kids, to the play ground, to the soccer field, to the grocery store like most of the rest of us. A good running $1,000 or $2,000 car does just as fine as a $50,000 car.

I see these guys and gals running around in these $40,000, $50,000 and even $60,000-dollar trucks, 4-Wheel Drive, jacked up, jacked down and it astounds me. If you are in construction I can see perhaps the need for one. If you are a cowboy, a rancher or a farmer, I can understand the need for one.

But if you are just driving back and forth down the freeway, the cost of insurance, the maintenance, the tires and batteries along with the payment is why they are broke.

If you want to know where your money is and why you are broke. Go look in the garage, or in the driveway or out on the street. That is where a significant amount of your money is.

79. NEVER LEASE A CAR.

Somebody please explain to me what the difference is between leasing a vehicle and buying one? Either one, the payment goes on for year after year after year.

Why in the world would you commit to a 3 or 5-year lease obligation? You don't need a $60,000-dollar BMW to drive around in. Just get what makes sense and what makes sense is a $2,000 safe, drivable vehicle that has 4 tires, a spare, a steering wheel, the wipers, seat belts, the heater and the air conditioner all work.

You are on a mission here and it doesn't involve trying to impress anybody or keeping up with the Johnsons. Your mission is to get "Free."

Having a lease payment on a vehicle has no resemblance of the definition of free. This is about having the "freedom" to do, go, have, buy, live where you want and having a lease payment just doesn't allow that sort of thing to happen.

Think about it.

80. NO RV PAYMENTS-NO BOAT PAYMENTS-NO FURNITURE PAYMENTS.

You are probably thinking is this guy going to give this a break? No, I am not. You want to be shackled all your life. Then go down to your nearest RV dealer, boat dealer and buy both a boat and an RV at the same time.

Furniture Stores are all over the place. What they sell is crap and cheap crap at that. They love the newlyweds, the foreigners and people who are broke.

If you are an aware individual, astute in all ways then when you are driving around, I am sure you have noticed the many acres of RV Storage facilities placed around your town. They are full of 1000's and 1,000's of RV's just sitting. Some in covered storages spaces. Some in carport type storage spaces. But most of them just sitting outside in the elements. Same for the boats. But, if you really want to see 1,000's and 1,000's of boats just sitting go to San Diego or another city on the water and go to the marinas. You will once again see 1,000's and 1,000's of boats sitting in the elements, rotting away. Never used and if they are, just a couple of times a year. It is mind boggling. It is this way all over the country. Great for the owners of the storage facilities.

The other thing that mystifies the mind is when it comes time for them to decide to sell the RV or the boat they want what the book says they are worth. They aren't worth much if anything at all. They have completely fallen apart, things don't work, they have discolored, and they are just one more piece of crap. They don't sell; they just sit and rot away.

There are RV's and boats that get used, taken care of and serve a purpose. Most don't. Often it is an emotional, spur of the moment purchase and it is a huge mistake.

Furniture is another one of those "purchases" in life that must be thought out. When you go to the furniture store and you purchase furniture on credit it is worth nothing by the time you get it home. It is even worse when you have the cash and pay cash for furniture. You could go by a $1,000 worth of new furniture, and have trouble selling it on Craig's List within an hour of getting it home for 25% of what you paid. If you had a garage sale you probably wouldn't even get 25%. If you need furniture why wouldn't you go to a garage sale or surf Craig's List or other on-line sites, or go to the Goodwill? Used furniture is all over the place and a lot of it is just like new. New is used when you get it home. Used is still used when you get it home.

This isn't about having a house full of crap. A garage even full of more crap. Or a couple of storage units full of still more crap. This is about learning to live within your means. Not having more than what is necessary and working to-wards a goal of getting "Free." If you need to think about this, then you obviously haven't got a "Life's Plan" you are following. You certainly aren't thinking about living a

"Free" life.

You probably need to spend a little bit more time in the bathroom.

81. GET YOUR FICO SCORE TO 750 PLUS AND KEEP IT THERE.

I am not somebody that has ever concentrated on or made it a mission to get his personal FICO score above 700. I know good credit is essential to leading a life that one can plan, manage and take care of things responsibly. A good FICO score makes that possible. I am not a big one on financing large purchases, living on credit and making credit the center of my life. I believe that cash is the way to go. If you don't have it, you certainly can't spend it. Chances are it is something you don't need, won't want in a couple of weeks and should have never bought in the 1st place.

If you have a good FICO score you can take an advantage of certain things. Zero interest car purchase might be one that comes to mind. Making a payment of principal only is certainly a lot smarter financial decision than a loan of 8 to 16%. The problem with any payment, interest free or not is it goes on forever.

A good credit rating sure goes a long way when it comes to purchasing a house. You are going to get punished and punished severely for your past credit and spending habits if they haven't been good. It can end up costing you a lot of money over a 15, 30 to 40-year period.

On the other side of the fence if you have learned to live within your means. Spending only what you have available to spend. By saving money every month, then the time will come when you don't even have to consider credit or a loan. You just walk in with your sack of cash and say OK, here is what I will give you, right now.

With a good, solid and determined outlook on life and living. Living and working your "Life's Plan" daily it gets to a point quick, you don't have to even consider credit or a loan. What also happens is you suddenly start to realize you really don't need that thing you are thinking about spending money on anyway.

All your needs are being met and things are just fine in your life. There is nothing better than waking up every day, knowing you are debt free. No payments of any kind and that savings account and investment portfolio just keeps getting bigger and bigger and bigger.

82. DO NOT LIVE ON CREDIT.

I am not referring to the type of credit that a business man needs to stay in business. Or a farmer or rancher or construction company needs to operate. I am also not talking the kind of credit that makes it possible to buy a house, with a 15-year mortgage or a vehicle with 0 % interest, those kinds of credit transactions.

I am talking about the kind of credit that is nothing but one big screwing. If you finance, get a loan or utilize a credit card to purchase a vehicle, an RV, furniture, dinners, vacations, buy food, go to Disney Land, take a cruise and you can't pay off the balance at the end of the month. You are not making a wise financial decision. It is nothing but a bad habit.

Once you start practicing only good habits, it is only a matter of time you will have more than enough cash to do anything you want within reason.

If you manage to save $50,000 in the next couple of years and you decide to take that $50,000 and go buy a new car and spend it all, you probably need to have your thought processes examined.

Over time, and time goes by fast, once you have $250,000 or even $500,000 saved, invested, liquid and protected by the ups and downs, then consideration might be given to having that nice new shiny piece of crap that by then it will probably cost you $75,000.

Credit cards are the death of many individuals and families. The kind of stress that is caused by having credit card debt is probably some of the worst. It causes havoc with couples, at work and in the family. It is just a very sickening feeling. Right up there with that kind of stress is medical bills. If you don't have good health insurance paying your medical bills, then you need to figure out a way to get healthy.

Now I fully understand that kids get sick, loved ones get sick and life can throw curve balls. That is life. It happens.

If you have over powering credit card debt, consumer debt and medical bills, a trip to the stationary store for the Chapter 7 filing packet is probably one of the 1st things you should do this next Saturday morning.

Getting "Free" is the goal here. Not creating a life where you are constantly behind on payments. The spare bedroom is full of boxes of junk. The garage is so full you can't park your car in it. The storage unit is full of stuff and you are thinking of getting another one. Look around you. Look at what is taking place. No money. Broke. Living paycheck to paycheck and there is box after box of crap all over the place.

Why do you think the retail industry is disappearing? It is because all of us have everything we need. We don't need any more crap. Some of us are getting smart and don't spend any money on anything anymore. If we do need something, we buy it used or get it for free.

The sooner you realize that spending money is a bad habit and saving money is a good habit the sooner you will be in the position to go outside, stand in the middle of the back yard, bend over and "Tell the World to Kiss Your Ass."

That is the goal here, not create a lifestyle that is built upon credit.

83. PAY CASH FOR EVERYTHING.

You would like to go out to dinner, take your wife or your honey, all the kids and their friends. Maybe Chucky Cheese would make sense for the kid's birthday party. I don't care what it is; it is going to cost money and sometimes a lot of money. The 1st question you should ask yourself when any one of these situations comes up, is does it make sense and do I have the cash to spend?

More than likely you do. But what happens if it is the last $350 you got until the end of the month and that is eight days away? Figure something else out. Every time you figure something else out it gets easier and easier every time to make the right decision.

Cash. Cash makes all the difference in the world when it comes to a feeling of security. If you never have any cash, then you obviously need to make some changes.

If you don't have the cash, don't even think about doing whatever it is that money needs to be spent. Just don't. That also becomes a good habit. There might be some temporary disappointment, but nothing lasts forever. If you start to budget, get that "Life's Plan" written down, follow it religiously, it won't be long, and you can go celebrate and reward yourself and your loved ones.

Pay cash. If you don't have it, wash the windows, clean the house, mow the lawn, trim the hedges, go for a walk or a bike ride and spend some quality time with your kids and your significant other.

Those sorts of things don't cost money.

84. RIDE THE BUS.

Having a vehicle is one of the biggest expenditures of cash monthly we all have. Some of us don't need to. Think about where all your money goes. They original purchase of the vehicle, the gas, the insurance, the cost of keeping it clean, the huge cost of keeping it running, the tires, the batteries the list is long. If you got a new one, then the warranty probably takes care of the cost of the maintenance. There are still all the other expenses. There are a lot of expenses associated with a vehicle that a lot of us just don't need.

This is one of those quick ways to get ahead. REAL QUICK. Consider your situation and what your short term, medium term and long-term goals are. You know what they are explicitly if you have done a "Life's Plan" and you are living it daily.

Go back thru your list of expenditures over the last six months or year, because that should also be available to you. Extract out of all those monies spent the cost of owning and operating that thing sitting in your garage or driveway or on the street. Take a good long look at what the total is.

Then ask yourself. Do I really need this car? If I took the bus, walked, rode my bike, moved closer to school or to work, called Uber of Lyft or we got rid of just one of the cars, look at what we could save. Maybe you got two or three of them, most families do. Most of us, if we are single have one.

I am single, and I have three. They are old, and they don't cost me much to have around. When I don't drive them for long periods of time, I have the insurance cancelled. A tool van, a Class C Motor Home and a one of a kind 1929 1 ½ Ton Chevy truck with a one of a kind camper on it.

As you are sitting there thinking of ways to cut expenses, there are ways to make the vehicle cost less. Gas is cheap now. But if you want to cut your gas expenses down in half, just drive half as much. There is also something else to think about. If you have made good decisions and you are in fact driving that $1,000 car then lots of times when work needs to be done on it and it costs more than $1,000 to fix it. You just go get another $1,000 car and give the title and the car to the junk yard. People will come and get them for free all the time.

Think about other ways to get around. Uber and Lyft have revolutionized the driving habits of a lot of us. Planned and done right you don't need a car.

I am saying it time after time. This is not about impressing anybody with the vehicle you drive. This is about impressing yourself with the size of your bank account and investment portfolio. This is about how soon are you going to be able to start your new journey in life, quit your job, go out in the middle of the forest and give the world the "Big Bend Over." You can do this anywhere. On the Golden Gate Bridge, down town Manhattan, in New Orleans, I don't care where you live, your goal is to get "Free."

85. WALK IF YOU CAN.

I know, I have talked about walking before. We are going to talk about it again because it is important. Not only from what it can do for your health and your attitude, but in the context of saving money. You can't get to where you are going with your "Life's Plan" if you don't constantly look for ways to save rather than spend. You might get lucky and fall into a situation like Abraham Piper did on 22 Words…but those kinds of situations don't happen very often.

Most of the time, the normal guy like you and I must work at getting to a place in life where we can control every aspect of our lives. It is possible.

Not everywhere, but most places in this country there is bus service, trains, car pool parking just about every conceivable way to get back forth to work you can think of is available if you just look for it and figure it out.

I know if your work place can be in multiple locations like a construction worker you often end up driving to work a different place every day. But if you work at the same place, day in and day out and you drive to work, alone, in your car. You are wasting money.

Walking to work, if it is close enough from a bus stop, or even close enough to get there within an hour's walk, can reap multiple benefits way above and beyond your wallet being a little fatter.

Car pooling is another way to share the expense. Taking the train, the tram or riding the bike is another way.

This quest you are on must be all out. It must be thought out, planned out and then executed. Nothing comes easy. Nothing is fair. Nobody is going to give you anything. That is what makes this living your own "Life's Plan" unique, different, challenging and worth it.

86. QUIT GOING OUT AND EATING. IT IS A WASTE OF MONEY.

You probably don't want to hear this but going out and eating is a waste of money. You might as well just flush that money down the toilet. In fact, that is exactly where it is going to end up the next day anyway.

Give me one solid, good, viable, makes sense reason for going out and eating all the time. Whether it is fast food, a Denney's or a top end restaurant. None of them make any sense to me.

Now I know there are birthdays, anniversaries, special occasions, promotions, getting fired, retiring, this and that and this, but to make it a habit of going out every day, several times a week doesn't make any sense. Why someone wouldn't make their own lunch and take it with them to work, good wholesome healthy food fascinates me.

Why you would go to a fast food restaurant day in and day out…. for your lunch…. you got to be nuts? Most of the time the food is not healthy, they are noisy, the food is bad, the service is even worse, people are rude, crude and disrespectful.

Think of the money you are wasting. It is a lot over a year's time. That gets back to keeping track of where you spend your money daily for six months. If this figure alone doesn't convince you do take your life's future into your own hands, nothing well. You are a lost cause.

There is no way you will be "Free", to a point to "Tell the World to Kiss Your Ass" if you are a go out and eater. You must be some kind of Stugoofid.

If you can master not going out and eating except on rare occasions, you will be successful in achieving your "Life's Plan" goals.

87. DO NOT DRINK EXPENSIVE COFFEES.

#87 is going to short and sweet. I am different that is for sure. Starbucks gets the crap kicked out of them all the time. Doesn't hurt them at all.

But I don't drink coffee. I haven't had a cup of coffee in well over 30 years. I do drink tea but not all the time. I have a cup of tea more for an excuse to sit down and plan my day or reflect on things.

There is a "exotic" coffee hut or location everywhere. They are prolific. Why? The demand is there. They make a lot of money. Some of the money they make is your money. It just doesn't make any sense to me to wait in line in your car or stand in line inside to spend all that money on something you are just going to piss away anyway. Can't be the taste, most of them taste like crap. Maybe it is the buzz?

But if you are keeping track of how you spend your money daily, for at least six months like we have talked about, then you probably are looking at a good amount of money going towards coffee. Stop it. You want to add a significant amount of money you save every month? Then change your approach to coffee and caffeine. I am not saying quit the coffee. I am saying manage it like you are about to do everything else in your life.

Think about this. Within an hour after you drink that expensive cup of coffee, you are going to be standing in front of the urinal or sitting on the pot and you could say to yourself, will there goes another $4.00. Maybe even $6.

88. BUY USED IF IT WORKS, FITS OR LOOKS GOOD.

I have hit on this one a little bit. Wonder why the some of the retail industry is failing except for Amazon? That is because we all have everything we need, in doubles. Amazon is just making it easier to accumulate more.

Some people are just tired of spending money and buying stuff they don't need or already have one or more of. They are the smart ones. Food and toilet paper are a constant, that is a given.

Wonder why you see all those new Goodwill stores being built all over the country? That is because people are giving away so much stuff that it is big business to sell it for a quarter or fifty cents on the dollar. I shop there all the time. I make sure it is on the blue tag days and senior discount days. I don't need or want much, but there is always something I am looking for to plug a hole or replace something. I am also constantly dropping stuff off to them as I work at weeding out what I don't need, don't use, don't touch and doesn't need to be lying around.

If you have a family and you are on the path to "Freedom" and living your "Life's Plan" a family outing to the second-hand stores, garage sales or the Goodwill store on a Saturday morning is a great way to spend family time together. Doesn't hurt your budget either. It could make the difference between saving another 5 or 10% of your gross pay every month, easily and maybe more.

From furniture, to clothes, to things to keep the house maintained, you name it; you can find it for pennies on the dollar. There is a reason sites like Craig's List have prospered.

The smart shoppers have gone to the "Used" market and stay away from the malls and retail outlets.

Going the used route is one of the best ways of getting to your end game, sooner than later. Once again, this isn't about how much money you can spend on crap. This is about how much money you don't spend on crap. This is about how soon you can get to your goal of being "Free."

Nothing else is more important in your life, except the safety and security of your family and yourself.

89. TRY TO SPEND A YEAR AND NOT BUY ANYTHING NEW.

Every now and then you can catch something on the internet about somebody who made the decision to not buy anything new for a year and what the positive outcome of that endeavor was. The concept of making the decision to not buy anything new for a year is by no means new.

If you are following you're "Life's Plan" to the "T", then you are already in the frame of mind to not be buying anything new. Hopefully by now it is already becoming a habit to resist the temptation to spend money. I can't think of one thing you would need new. Tell me what that is?

We all now and then surf Craig's List. If you can't find it on Craig's it hasn't been invented or made yet.

If you haven't ever been in an updated "Rehab" store run by the Habitat for Humanity folks you need to stop by one. These days that is also becoming big business. If you shop around and you are patient, you can just about pick up new building products/or like new at the "Rehab" stores and stay out of Lowes and Home Depot.

Once again, this is not about today. This is about tomorrow, down the road and not too far in the distance. This is about that "getting free" thing I keep referring to. You need to shut your eyes and imagine it. The vision of it is different for all of us. Neither I nor anyone else can put that vision in your mind's eye. It must be you. You know what it is. We are all different in so many ways but are also so alike in so many ways.

Saving money by not buying anything new, unless you absolutely need to, means more goes into your savings account and investment portfolio. You have no idea until you get to the age where the money in the bank, or where ever it is, is what makes the bending over and giving the world the "moon" the difference.

Not enough money or worse yet no money…. means no "freedom."

90. START AN LLC TO LESSEN THE TAX BURDEN.

Along with creating another source of income other than your weekly/bi weekly pay check or even income from your business, it sometimes makes sense to have an LLC. An LLC can create another avenue for deducting business expenses, therefore lessening the tax burden. The less taxes you owe, the more you can save.

LLC's are a great easy, inexpensive way to create deductions for a business. You can grow worms and sell them in your front yard. It doesn't make any difference what it is.   If it is something that can create income, then it is something that also can create some expenses.

The secret here is to make sure it is something that can create more income than expenses.

I make a complete disclaimer here; I am no tax authority or accountant. But my experience has taught me this much. Any time you can figure out an avenue to pay fewer taxes, legally, the better off you are in the long run. There is nothing worse than getting to April 10th and finding out you owe the IRS and you don't have the cash.

91. START A SECOND SMALL BUSINESS.

Number 91 will be another short one. Depending on whom you are and how you manage your time, having a second small business might make sense.

The possibilities are endless. Making an additional $1,000 per month above and beyond your expenses doesn't sound like much. Take that $1,000 times 12 months. That is $12,000. That is a lot of money to add to the savings account and the investment portfolio. 10 years and you are talking a lot of money. 10 years goes by so fast it is like tomorrow.

Don't forget, you have a lot time on your hands because you aren't watching TV anymore. You aren't going out and eating anymore. You aren't spending time at the Mall spending money you shouldn't.

Why not find something else that you are good at or interest you and make some money at it.

92. DO NOT BE IGNORANT OF THE TAX CODES.

You certainly don't need to have an MBA in accounting to have some knowledge of how much you are going to be paying in taxes to the IRS or the state you live in. Planning can make all the difference in the amount you get back. Good planning can also lessen the burden of what you might end up owing.

Being aware of what it takes to "legitimately" pay as little as possible in taxes is only prudent and responsible. There is no question that it should be part of your "Life's Plan." You can't have too many ways to achieve your goals. Knowing how the tax thing works is just as important as throwing the TV in the dumpster.

If you are serious, chances are in your town there is a Junior College or a school that you could take a class on accounting and taxes. Wouldn't hurt to know as much as you can.

Getting smart on taxes will help when you start to implement your plan of creating multiple streams of income. What kind of corporation, what kind of business identity, there are all kinds of ways to lessen you tax burden. If you don't know, you don't know. Find out. It is another one of those sure-fire ways of getting there sooner than later.

But, if you are one of those stugoofids, then you don't care whether you get there or not.

93. DO NOT PAY FOR A SERVICE IF YOU CAN DO IT YOURSELF

I hear people all the time say they just had the maid come in. The maid? Who are you that you are so-o-o-o busy you have a maid? Let's see now. The maid, the landscaper, the pool service company, the tree trimmer, the window washer, assuming the maid doesn't do windows and probably doesn't, the car washer at work or in the driveway, the list is endless.

There are folks who are way in over their head in time commitments, kids to and from school/daycare, work, working two jobs, volunteering, committees, relationships, this list is endless also. But!

If the TV has in fact ended up in the dumpster, or on the sidewalk with a free sign around its neck, or you gave it to someone you don't like or sold it, you got a lot of time on your hands you never had before. Your busy, or were, but I'll bet you were never too busy to not get a couple of hours of TV in a day. Then when you have cut out all the going out and eating and the time spent in line at the Starbucks, you got nothing but time on your hands now.

How about saving some money? This is money that can go right into the savings account and your investment portfolio. Great family thing to mow the lawn, do the landscaping, wash the windows, trim the hedges and the trees, clean the pool, the hot tub and wash the cars together. Not everybody owns a house and has these sorts of things to do. If you live in a condo or rent, then you don't have these time-consuming tasks to perform. But there are other things you can look for to save money. Find them.

Doing this sort of thing has to be looked upon as fun. That's right fun. Or exercise. Or family time. Or if for no other reason, it means that it is going to get you there faster. Only you know where there is. If you make it your ambition and your mission, it will start to come into focus and become clearer and clearer as the weeks and months go by. And they will go by. Very fast.

94. GIVE YOUR SELF A RAISE BY CUTTING OUT THE FLUFF.....ASK FOR A RAISE FROM YOUR BOSS/WORK.

Fluff. It is everywhere. In every dollar you spend there is some fluff. You should by now know what that fluff is. You have done your six months to a year of keeping track of where every penny you spend has gone. Fluff. It should be running off the page.

Now that you know what it is, you have done your budget and you are living within your means, there is no more fluff. The fluff has turned into cash, which should go directly into your savings account or your investment portfolio.

That is a significant raise right there. Now go to your boss if you work for a paycheck and sit your boss down, your manager and tell him you deserve a raise. Tell him how much. Make it reasonable. I don't care if it is only .50 cents. That all goes directly into your savings account and your investment portfolio after taxes.

If you are a Small Business Owner, or a Big Business Owner there is always lots of fluff. No matter how big or how small the business is, fluff is everywhere.

Turn that fluff into a bonus. You were going to spend it anyway.

In your "Life's Plan" you should have an exit plan. That exit plan includes when, how much is going to be there for your retirement, the selling of the business, the passing on of the business to someone in the family or the creation of an employee owned business. It doesn't make any difference what it is. What you think it is today might not be what it is tomorrow. But I can absolutely guarantee you one thing; the day is coming much sooner than you think. Some people ride it all the way to the casket or the furnace. If that was part of their "Life's Plan" good for them.

Once you have determined where all that money was going, tighten up, take a good look at everything and try to figure out where you can find more "fluff."

Remember this very important thing about life. It never stops for any one. It just keeps going by day after day. This type of living, sacrificing if that is what you want to call it, isn't going to last forever. There is nothing more gratifying and satisfying than knowing you have achieved some short-term goals. Those short-term goals turn into long term achievements. It is rewarding. It is uplifting. It is healthy, and it will get you to the finish line all that much sooner. The finish line is a moving target.

But at some point, in time, you turn the corner and there is the finish line. You cross it. Your life changes significantly.

You are here, there, everywhere "Telling the World to Kiss Your Ass" and living life to the fullest.

95. BE WARY OF ANY KIND OF INSURANCE.

This is one of those topics I am no good at. I hate insurance. Some insurance is necessary. Some insurance isn't necessary. There are a lot of folks over the years that wished they would have had flood or fire insurance. They didn't. They could have but they choose not to. Fine line to walk and sometimes it saves money and sometimes it cost big time.

Health insurance is a biggie these days and what a mess. I have no experience or comments here that would help any-one. I am plugged into the VA because I am 100% Service Disabled and that is where my knowledge lies. If you want-ed me to comment on that part of my life's experiences I would have nothing but good to say.

Life insurance is another one of those topics of conversations that can only be discussed with folks that are knowledgeable. Don't make life insurance an impulse or an emotional deci-sion. Make the decision based upon the best of information, the best of intentions and the best experience you can find to help make that decision.

Car insurance you must have. If you drive without it, that is like smoking. You aren't making the wisest of decisions to drive without car insurance. A lot of folks do. They either can't afford it or don't think the next accident is going to involve them.

If you are in business, then the list of insurances needed becomes an entirely different discussion. But, it is another one of those necessities. You can't be in business without it.

Shopping for insurance is an art. It takes time, it is stressful, and it can save a lot of money if you shop around. Take the time. It could end up being a big part of the fluff you find. Not only in your personal life but in your business life.

Anytime you get into the realm of "commissioned earnings" you must be very careful. The guy or gal selling you the insurance might have a different objective. They might have a mortgage payment, rent payment, car payment, credit card payment due or their kids need shoes. They need to....no... they must make a sale. If you don't think for a minute they have their best interest in mind, verses yours, you need to go look in the mirror and wonder who the "stugoofid" really is.

Insurance is no fun. But it is part of the budget. It is part of "it is what it is." Make it happen. Keep it simple. Accept it and manage it properly.

96. RENTING SOMETIMES CAN BE MORE FINAN-CIALLY ADVANTAGOUS THAN BUYING.

I refer to renting in the context of everything. Whether it is an apartment, a condo, a house, half of a duplex a town house, a paint machine, a jack hammer, a car, a truck or anything you need. What you can rent today is everything. Then again, lots of times depending on the circumstances it might make sense to just buy it outright, keep it, sell it or trade it.

You can search out and find many articles about renting your living space versus owning that space. Owning a house can be expensive. Just because they tell you, you can own for what you are paying in rent doesn't mean that makes sense. What they don't tell you is what all the taxes, maintenance, insurances, fences needing fixed, roofs replaced, septic systems replaced, on and on and on can go the expenditures necessary just to maintain a residence, let alone upgrade one. Not just once, but it goes on forever.

If it is time to paint the house, you might be surprised how much money you can save by painting it yourself. A bid of $6,500 can turn into a cost of $2,700 by renting the ladders and paint machine. Those type of examples can be endless.

One nice thing about renting the living space is you can give a 30-day notice. Move out and that is it. If your wife is badgering you about fixing the leak in the kitchen sink, tell her to "Call the Landlord." If you have signed a lease, that becomes another matter all together. A lease is construed as a legal and binding contract. Now leases can be renegotiated. You can terminate for cause. The secret to a lease is have an escape clause and don't let it go beyond a year.

With a mortgage, it is impossible to call up the mortgage holder and tell them that you have had it. You are not going to be making any more payments. You are giving them a 30-day notice. Doesn't work that way. You can do that but know that phone call will cause all kinds of grief. Unless you have plans to file Chapter 7.

When it comes to making one of the biggest financial decisions you will ever make in your life, think, think and think again about what the ramifications are. Compare renting versus buying over a 5 to 10-year period if you can look down the road that far on what the difference is in cost.

Remember. Your goal right now is to complete your mission. Fulfilling every aspect of your "Life's Plan."

Only the safety, security and health of you and your family is what is important. Put the well being of yourself and your family first. If you are stressed out because you haven't been able to buy a house yet, do your homework. You might just find out you are where you should be.

97. GET EFFICIENT.

This is a great one. This is probably my most favorite. I could expound up on this getting efficient for a long time.

One of the best ways to get efficient is get your ass out of bed. Not just one day a week, but every day. Perhaps you are already one who rises early. Good for you.

The 2nd best way to get efficient is once you are out of bed; don't waste any time in getting with it.   An awful lot of productive time is wasted in the first couple hours of the day. Which by the way in my opinion is the most productive part of the day. This doesn't mean you can't go out on the porch and watch the sun come up over a cup of coffee or a cup of tea or a cup of hot chocolate. Probably one of the few times I would agree with having a cup of coffee.

Once you have done your 10-minute routine, hit it.

Exercising, meditating, yoga, walking, running, bike riding, something that involves physical activity is what starts the day out right. When I lived up on East Lake those 2 ½ years I use to go out and trim trees just for something to do. I ended up trimming acres of jack pines. Looked like a park. Great exercise and being out there listening to the birds was one of the greatest experiences of my life. That is where, as I have said, the idea for this book came from.

I never start a day without a list of things to do. Never. One of the greatest daily satisfactions I have is looking at the list at the end of the day and seeing that not only did I accomplish what I had set out to do, but more. You can't top that.

It is the number one way I have found out to continue down my path…being efficient. My "Life's Plan" is a work in progress. It changes constantly like the waves hitting the beach. It flows back and forth with the changing challenges of living in a complex world. Starting your day out knowing what your capabilities are and what your limitations are is invaluable.

Perhaps the greatest gain in life is self-knowledge. For if you do not know yourself and what others think of you, rightly or wrongly, it is difficult or almost impossible to navigate thru a complicated world. We all, each and every one of us, waste an incredible amount of energy….merely to fight our way through the perversity in ourselves.

I didn't write these last two lines, somebody else did. But read them again.

Where are you going? Without the self-knowledge that is ever so important, you will never get there.

98. IF YOU HAVEN'T TOUCHED IT IN A YEAR, CHANCES ARE YOU NEVER WILL. SELL IT, GIVE IT AWAY, OR THROW IT AWAY.

Stuff. Junk. Crap. Things. Most of us have it all and then some. 20 pairs of socks, 10 pairs of shoes, 40 pairs of pants, it is a lot of stuff and it must go some place. My second wife had enough "things" for two, if not three households. Most of it we bought new. Some of it was given to us. Some of us like garage sales, 2nd hand stores. We just never seemed to have enough stuff.

I used to have garage sales all the time, then would go out and buy more crap. Not anymore.

The worst part of it was, I would pay $10 bucks for something at a garage sale and a month later sell it at one of my garage sales for $2 bucks. That is insane.

Stuff takes a lot of time. Stuff is stressful. It is in the closets, the garage, the storage shed, the barn, the storage unit, the attic, the back of the truck, in the trunk of the car; it is all over the place.

Get rid of it. Every bit of it and then some. The reason isn't necessarily what small amount of cash it might bring you. It is part of the idea of getting free of it. There is that free thing again.

If you haven't touched it in a year or used it, chances are you aren't going to. Now I am not talking about the paint sprayer, or the weed whacker, things like that. I am talking about the crap.

Have a garage sale, donate it, give it away or put it on the sidewalk with a free sign.

99. THINK ABOUT THE DECISION TO SPEND AN UNUSUAL AMOUNT OF MONEY FOR 24 HOURS.

This is important. When I am going to go to town, which is not very often, I have a list of each place I am going to go and spend money. I make that list for days and sometimes weeks before going. Then I look at it the day before I do go to town. Then the day I go I revise the list and half of it never happens. Want to know why? Because most of what I had on the list to spend money on was not necessary. I just thought I might like to do that or get that or have that thing that costs money.

You can't think for 24 hours if you need to stop and fill the gas tank up. But you should do a list for almost anything you are going to go out and spend money on. I can't imagine going to the grocery store without a list. I never go to the grocery store hungry either. Never. I hardly every buy anything that is not on the list. No impulse buying. I know what I need and that is it. There is a huge difference between what you need and what you want.

What I am referring to on the 24-hour thing is spending money on big ticket items. Going out to dinner with the family or honey is a big one. A weekend at the beach or to the mountains is another one. A new bedroom set is always needed. I know you are never going to ever again consider a new TV. Buying new furniture for any room in the house is one of the biggest wastes of money there is.

Going to Las Vegas is another one of the wastes of money I have never understood. We lived in Vegas for 12 years and it is without a doubt, the last place in the world I would go for a vacation.

Taking the time to rationalize the need to spend money becomes a habit. It is another one of those good habits that is a result of doing the "Life's Plan." Anytime you are going to spend money it should be discussed and talked about.

If you are single or married just go in the bathroom and stand in front of the mirror and have the conversation. Just look yourself in the eye and ask, "should I spend the money on this or not." If you are serious about following your "Life's Plan" the answer is probably going to be a simple and decisive NO.

August 25, 2017, on Yahoo News. "8 out of 10 American workers say they are living paycheck to paycheck to make ends meet."

Need I say more?

100. REMEMBER THIS EVERY DAY; SOMEONE OUT THERE IS TRYING TO TAKE EVERY DIME YOU HAVE.

Life is one big casino. Casino's are in business to take all your money. They don't care what the consequences are for you. They are ruthless, and they are serious. And they are very good at it.

Life is no different. Nobody told you it was going to be fair. It isn't. If you don't get in control, you will be like the 8 out of 10 other workers in this country who live paycheck to paycheck.

It is the same with banks, credit card companies, finance companies, insurance companies and for sure the car industry. The States and the Federal Government are there on the corner with their hand out also. They all want your money. All of it. Then to make sure they keep taking your money once they have got all your cash, they give you CREDIT.

You walk out that front door everyday and you walk into the war zone. The financial war zone. They are all waiting out there to take your money.

You can win the battle day in and day out. Just don't spend any money. They biggest test is to walk out the door in the morning with $100 bill. Then when you get home put that $100 on your dresser. Do that day in and day out with the same $100 bill. You do that and do it for a month....you will win the war.

It is a given that there is gas to be bought, milk to bring home and the kids need shoes. But all that kind of money that needs to be spent is already allocated and in the budget. I am talking about the cash. The cash that you are giving to everybody. Goes back to why in the world would you work all week long and then give it all to somebody else? Bad enough you don't give yourself any. But to do this continually is sheer lunacy.

Take a walk with me again on this. Let's go in the bathroom. Shut the door, put the toilet seat down and here we are once again. Sit down on the toilet, close your eyes and envision being "Free." Financially free. Debt free. You are 52 years old, the kids are out of the house and you and your wife have $1.5 million in the portfolio and tomorrow is the day.

The day you finally "Tell the World to Kiss Your Ass."

Now stand up and look in the mirror. Are you prepared to make a commitment to yourself and get with the "Life's Plan"? Are you strong enough and committed enough to live up to the commitment and not disappoint yourself anymore? There is nobody else going to do it for you.

This is a defining moment.

101. HAPPINESS AND BEING "FREE" ARE A STATE OF MIND IMMERSED IN REALITY!

These are two things that you can't fake, hide behind, try to fool everybody let alone yourself. It is or it isn't. Period. Of course, I would like to think you realize that if you don't have your health, then neither "Happiness" or being "Free" are going to be where you end up.

I believe at this stage of life, that these two things are ultimately what we all strive for in one form or another depending on our point of view and the way we live our lives.

I also firmly believe, they can be planned, and they can be made to happen. It is all a matter of how soon and how diligently we planned our "Life's Plan" and how well we executed over a period of time that "Life's Plan."

So many people are pissed off today, angry, unsettled, tired of the rat race day in and day out. Tired of working pay check to pay check and living a life of destitute just over the horizon. This is all, in my estimation, just poor planning and going with the flow.

There are people, and I know some who have it all, but just won't stop to live their live in a state of "happiness and being free." They have no concept of "when is enough...enough."

A day turns into a week, a week turns in to a month, then

a month turns into a year, a year turns in to 5 years, then 5 years turns in to 20, 20 years turns into 50 years. It all goes by so fast, most people have the attitude day in and day out "it is what it is" why fight it or attempt to change it.

Yes, there are things one has no control over and for sure "it is what it is." But most things in our lives, we do have control over and once we learn how to exercise that control with our thought processes and practicing the "5 P's" then we get in control and we can make "it is what it is" exactly what we want it to be.

I have mentioned it several times in past pages, "when is enough, enough?." When is enough "too much"? When is it "not enough"? No one can answer that for us as individuals. They try. Society puts a tremendous amount of pressure on all of us to create circumstances that never allows to answer any of those questions.

Your "Life's Plan" in my opinion can. You lay it out, you work it as time goes on, you adjust it to circumstances. You maneuver it as your life's experiences teach you things about yourself. As family situations change and it ends up being just the two of you then there are going to be more changes take place in how you pursue the goals of your "Life's Plan."

But ultimately, the main goal is to get "Free", be content and happy with your life and most of all be able to when the appropriate time is right: "Tell the World to Kiss Your Ass."

ABOUT THE AUTHOR

DAVID H. SCOTT served in Vietnam from 1966 to 1968, extending 2 different tours of duty for a total of 26 months. He spent his 19th, 21st and 22nd birthdays in Vietnam. His 1st 12-month tour of duty was as an Infantry Soldier in combat with the 101st Airborne. His 1st extension was for 6 months to be Lt. General Rosson's personal driver. The 2nd 6-month extension was as General Rosson's driver and then became Lt. General Rosson's personal enlisted aide.

Upon Lt. General Rosson's rotation from Vietnam, Mr. Scott became Lt. General Stillwell's personal enlisted aide until he finally went home for good.

After the war Mr. Scott worked construction and owned businesses. A fireplace shop, a painting business, several construction companies, a Service Disabled Veteran Owned Small Business, superintended projects, a motel and RV Park, an energy conservation retrofit lighting business, mortgage loan officer, sold real estate, was a Mayor of a small Eastern Oregon community.

He married in his mid-20's, had five children 2 boys and 3 girls. The first boy Brad drowned in an irrigation ditch in Bend, Oregon at the age of 16 months.

Mr. Scott is a 100% Service Disabled Veteran.

He has been sober as of 2018 for 21 years after getting 9 DUI's over a period of 27 years. Something he is not proud of, but he is grateful for his sobriety and finally figuring out how to be an adult and live a full life.

Mr. Scott is an avid solo kayaker, kayaking long trips. He also river rafts extensively.

In 2014, he kayaked/river rafted the Snake River in the Western United States from Flagg Ranch, Wyoming to the Columbia River in Washington a total of 1,200 miles, 42 days.

In 2016, he kayaked the Yellowstone River, starting at Gardiner, Montana, to the Missouri River west of Williston, North Dakota, to the Mississippi at St. Louis, Illinois then on down to Baton Rouge, Louisiana. Close to 3,000 miles, 100 days.

In 2017, he kayaked the Yukon River, leaving Whitehorse, Yukon and ended his trip prematurely at the Native Village of Grayling, Alaska because his thumbs and his thumb joints gave out on him. A total of 1,600 miles, 55 days, with less than 250 miles to go.

He is also the author of:
The Generals Driver
A Vietnam Soldier Remembering

He resides nowhere and everywhere. He spends time in Bend, OR. He river rafts, kayaks, walks, paints and is grateful for his health and his full life.